Sexuality Education Curricula

The Consumer's Guide

Roberta J. Ogletree, HSD, CHES
Joyce V. Fetro, PhD, CHES
Judy C. Drolet, PhD, CHES, FASHA
Barbara A. Rienzo, PhD, CHES, FASHA

with **Christine E. Beyer, MEd,**
and **Nancy L. LaCursia, MS, CHES**

ETR ASSOCIATES
Santa Cruz, California
1994

ETR Associates (Education, Training and Research) is a nonprofit organization committed to fostering the health, well-being and cultural diversity of individuals, families, schools and communities. The publishing program of ETR Associates provides books and materials that empower young people and adults with the skills to make positive health choices. We invite health professionals to learn more about our high-quality publishing, training and research programs by contacting us at P.O. Box 1830, Santa Cruz, CA 95061-1830, 1-800-321-4407.

Published by ETR Associates, P.O. Box 1830,
Santa Cruz, California 95061-1830

Printed in the United States of America
Designed by Cliff Warner
10 9 8 7 6 5 4 3 2 1
Title No. 567

Library of Congress Cataloging-in-Publication Data

Sexuality education curricula : the consumer's guide /
    Roberta J. Ogletree ... [et al.].
        p.   cm.
    Includes bibliographical references.
    ISBN 1-56071-354-2
    1. Sex instruction—United States—Curricula—
Evaluation. I. Ogletree, Roberta J.
    HQ57.5.A3S4897   1994
    613.9'07—dc20   93-46042

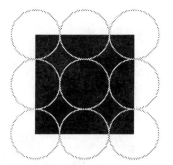

Contents

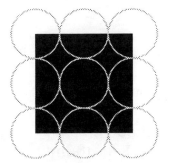

Programs Included in *The Consumer's Guide*

Level 4

Special Education

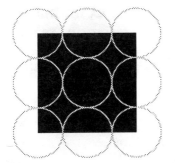

Acknowledgments

The following individuals or groups of individuals assisted in making this publication a reality. The authors would like to express their appreciation to

All the professionals, both practitioners and researchers, who continue to develop, implement and evaluate sexuality education curricula in hopes of addressing the diverse needs of today's youth.

The publishers who contributed copies of their curricula for inclusion in this guide.

The Sex Information and Education Council of the United States (SIECUS), whose National Task Force of health, education, and sexuality professionals developed the guidelines used as a basis for selection of attributes assessed in this review.

Cindy Clark, for her early work in identifying potential sources of published sexuality education curricula.

The Department of Health Education at Southern Illinois University at Carbondale for its support throughout the curriculum review process.

Michael Emerson and Amy Kate Bailey for their assistance in contacting publishers and following up on the "nitty-gritty" details.

And, finally, to Kay Clark, for her technical support, guidance and willingness to accept the challenge of helping to create this guide.

A critical element of this consumer's guide was the examination and evaluation of the curricula by consumers, i.e., classroom teachers, health educators and special education teachers. A heartfelt thanks to the following reviewers whose efforts made this project especially useful to those for whom it is intended:

Marcia Abell (Middle School Teacher)
Dongola Unit #66, Dongola, Illinois
Certification: Physical Education K–12; Health 6–12
Years Experience: 18

Susan Arndt (High School Teacher)
Booker High School, Sarasota, Florida
Certification: Health, Biology 9–12
Years Experience: 24

Eric Childs (High School Teacher)
Palm Beach High School, Palm Beach Gardens, Florida
Certification: Health, Physical Education 9–12
Years Experience: 9

Jacqueline Cooper (Elementary School Teacher)
George Peabody School, San Francisco, California
Certification: General Elementary
Years Experience: 36

Kathy A. Escue (Middle School Teacher)
Giant City School, Carbondale, Illinois
Certification: Physical Education 6–8
Years Experience: 14

Heather Favale (Graduate Student)
Southern Illinois University, Carbondale, Illinois
Certification: Health 6–12
Years Experience: Student Teaching

Linda Garden (Elementary School Teacher)
Miraloma School, San Francisco, California
Certification: General Elementary
Years Experience: 25

David L. Gename (High School Teacher)
Carbondale Community High School-East, Carbondale, Illinois
Certification: Health, Physical Education K–12
Years Experience: 22

Lorie Mesches Goldberg (High School Teacher)
Palm Beach High School, West Palm Beach, Florida
Certification: Home Economics 9–12
Years Experience: 10

Emily Graig (Special Education Teacher)
Dongola Unit #66, Dongola, Illinois
Certification: Special Education (Learning Disabled, Behaviorally
    Disturbed, Emotionally/Mentally Handicapped)
Years Experience: 7

Kathryn A. Kupecz (Middle School Teacher)
Cherry Creek Schools, Englewood, Colorado
Certification: Health, Physical Education K–12
Years Experience: 8

Shelly Lange (Middle School Teacher)
Central District 301 Middle School, Burlington, Illinois
Certification: Physical Education, Biology 6–12
Years Experience: 6

Therese McLaughlin (Elementary School Teacher)
Jose Ortega School, San Francisco, California
Certification: General Elementary, Special Education K–5
Years Experience: 8

Rosalina Nagle (Elementary Resource Teacher—Special Education)
Thomas Elementary School, Carbondale, Illinois
Certification: Special Education (Learning Disabled/Behaviorally Disturbed/Emotionally Mentally Handicapped)
Years Experience: 12

Constanza Pedraza (AIDS Education Specialist)
School Health Programs Department, San Francisco, California
Certification: General Elementary, Bilingual Education (Pending)
Years Experience: 5

Dennis Ragan (High School Teacher)
Carbondale Community School-West, Carbondale, Illinois
Certification: Health, Physical Education 6–12
Years Experience: 13

Meyla Ruwin (Health Resource Teacher—Secondary Level)
School Health Programs Department, San Francisco, California
Certification: Health Science, Physical Education, Biology 6–12
Years Experience: 8

Jody Smith (High School Teacher)
Charleston High School, Charleston, Illinois
Certification: Health, Physical Education 6–12
Years Experience: 11

Linda Telles (Elementary School Teacher)
Junipero Serra School, San Francisco, California
Certification: General Elementary
Years Experience: 30

Dusty Twining (High School Teacher)
New Directions Alternative High School, Sarasota, Florida
Certification: Psychology, Sociology, History 6–12
Years Experience: 8

Joyce Vickery (Health Education Consultant)
Sarasota, Florida
Certification: Health K–12
Years Experience: 16

Diane Waterfall (High School Teacher)
Palm Beach Lakes High School, West Palm Beach, Florida
Certification: Home Economics 9–12
Years Experience: 10

Harry Winkler (High School Teacher)
Forest Hill High School, West Palm Beach, Florida
Certification: Health 9–12
Years Experience: 21

Barbara Ginn Yarnall (High School Teacher)
Venice High School, Venice, Florida
Certification: Physical Education 6–12
Years Experience: 18

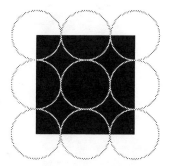

Introduction

Over the past twenty years, in response to increases in sexuality-related behaviors among young people, numerous sexuality education curricula with a variety of goals and objectives have been developed for students at all grade levels.

A number of questions arise as school administrators, curriculum specialists, classroom teachers and others make decisions about selecting sexuality education curricula for implementation in their school districts. What content should be included in the curriculum and is it appropriate for the developmental level of the students? Does the curriculum use skill-building strategies that have been shown to be effective in prevention programs? Does the curriculum employ a variety of instructional strategies to address individual needs and learning styles? Is the curriculum culturally sensitive? Can it be implemented without additional teacher training? And so on.

The Consumer's Guide provides information about 26 school-based sexuality education curricula. It will assist administrators, program planners, and teachers as they review published curricula to determine if they meet the needs of the school district.

Every effort was made to identify, select and include available curricula that met the criteria described below. Nevertheless, it is possible some programs were missed. And some publishers elected not to have their curricula included. Appendix B lists curricula not included in the guide, and gives the reasons why.

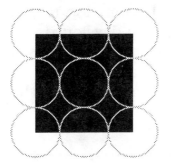

Developing *The* Consumer's Guide

A systematic approach was used in the development of *The Consumer's Guide*. The following sections describe the process of selection and evaluation of each curriculum included in the guide.

Identifying Available Curricula

To identify published sexuality education curricula, a computerized library search was conducted using the Education Resources Information Center (ERIC). In addition, resource lists from the Sex Information and Education Council of the United States (SIECUS), the Comprehensive Health Information Database (CHID), and other sources of sexuality education curricula were secured and reviewed. From this review, 68 sexuality education curricula were identified.

Selecting Curricula

To narrow the number of curricula reviewed in this guide, the following criteria were applied:

- The curriculum was school-based.
- The curriculum was published and/or revised since 1985.
- The curriculum was available for review.
- The curriculum did not focus on a single sexuality issue (e.g., sexual abuse, sexually transmitted disease, HIV infection).

Publishers were called to determine whether information related to selection criteria was accurate, to identify newly developed curricula that may have been omitted from lists, and to secure copies of curricula for review and permission for inclusion in the guide. A list of curricula excluded from this guide and the reasons for their exclusion is included in Appendix B.

Developing Curriculum Descriptions

After careful review of introductory material in the curriculum and the contents of each curriculum package, a one- to two-page description was written, including key information such as title and author, year of development (with latest revision), target grade levels, length (in number of lessons), and cost. The curriculum description presents a general overview of the curriculum focus, lesson format and contents of the curriculum package. The name, address and telephone number of the publisher are included.

Identifying Attributes of Curricula

Guidelines for Comprehensive Sexuality Education: Kindergarten–12th Grade (National Guidelines Task Force, 1991) and *Sexuality Education Within Comprehensive School Health Education* (Neutens, Drolet, Dushaw and Jubb, 1991) were used to identify key content and skill-building strategies to be included in the Attributes of Curricula matrixes.

The SIECUS *Guidelines* were developed by a task force of leading health, education, and sexuality professionals and present a comprehensive approach to sexuality education through a carefully constructed scope and sequence of developmentally appropriate key concepts. (A copy of these guidelines is available from the Sex Information and Education Council of the United States, 130 West 42nd Street, Suite 2500, New York, NY 10036; telephone (212) 819-9770.)

Sexuality Education Within Comprehensive Health Education was written by the Council on Sexuality Education of the American School Health Education as a guide to teachers, administrators, school board members and parents/caregivers in the planning and implementation of successful sexuality education programs. It suggests age-appropriate concepts, content and student activities. (A copy of this publication is available from the American School Health Association, 7263 State Route 43, P.O. Box 708, Kent, OH; telephone (216) 678-1601.)

Content

The SIECUS *Guidelines* identify specific topic areas with appropriate content for different age groups (developmental messages). Based on the publisher's target grade levels, each curriculum was reviewed for inclusion of age-appropriate content.

Initially, the four authors worked in pairs to determine if content attributes were addressed in the curriculum. Then, assessments from both pairs of authors were compared. When discrepancies occurred, the curriculum content was reviewed a third time by one of the authors.

Readers should refer to the two publications listed above for age-appropriate developmental messages. The content categories used are as follows:

- Puberty
- Body Image
- Gender Roles
- Reproductive Anatomy/Physiology
- Conception and Birth
- Sexual Identity and Orientation
- Relationships
- Parenting
- Sexual Expression
- STD Transmission
- HIV Transmission
- Abstinence
- Pregnancy Prevention
- STD Prevention
- HIV Prevention
- Sexual Exploitation
- Reproductive Health

Philosophy

Each curriculum was examined to determine its underlying philosophy(ies) related to sexuality. In this assessment, the authors primarily relied heavily on statements made by the curriculum writer about the purpose of the curriculum and its goals and objectives. The validity of these statements was further assessed by reviewing developmental messages addressed and student activities included.

The philosophy was defined by the following categories:

- Promotes Healthy Sexuality
- Promotes Responsibility for Decisions
- Promotes Abstinence
- Promotes Using Protection if Sexually Active
- Philosophy Not Clear

Skill-Building Strategies

The SIECUS *Guidelines* identify specific personal and interpersonal skills necessary for healthy sexuality. Moreover, evaluation of prevention programs over the past twenty years have identified key skill-building strategies that should be included in sexuality education curricula. (For more detail about effectiveness of specific prevention programs, see: Alcohol, Drug Abuse and Mental Health Administration, 1990; Bell and Battjes, 1987; Botvin and Wills, 1985; Eisen, Zellman and McAllister, 1990; Fetro, 1992; Flay, 1985; Glasgow and McCaul, 1985; Howard and McCabe, 1991; Kirby, Barth, Leland and Fetro, 1991; Kumpfer, 1990; Lando, 1985; Schaps, DiBartolo, Moskowitz, Palley and Churgin, 1981; Schinke, Blythe and Gilchrist, 1981).

Inclusion of the following skill-building strategies was assessed for each sexuality education curriculum:

- Examining Personal Values
- Increasing Self-Awareness/Building Self-Esteem
- Examining Influences on Decisions
- Identifying Consequences of Decisions
- Addressing Peer Norms
- Examining Perceived Pregnancy Risk
- Examining Perceived STD/HIV Risk
- Accessing Community Resources

- Building General Communication Skills
- Building Assertiveness Skills
- Building Refusal Skills
- Building Conflict-Management Skills
- Building Decision-Making Skills
- Building Planning/Goals-Setting Skills

Teaching Strategies

To meet the individual needs and learning styles of students and to provide opportunities for personal and social skill building, a wide variety of instructional strategies is necessary. The following teaching strategies were assessed in each sexuality education curriculum:

- Groundrules
- Anonymous Question Box
- Teacher Lecture
- Large-Group Discussion
- Student Worksheets
- Journals/Story Writing
- Cooperative Learning/Small Groups
- Case Studies/Scenarios
- Skills Practice and Rehearsal
- Audiovisual Materials
- Community Speakers/Involvement
- Peer Helper Component
- Parent/Guardian Involvement

Evaluating the Curricula

The Evaluation of Curricula matrix was completed after the Attributes of Curricula matrixes were finalized. Evaluation categories and the criteria underlying them were selected based on a review of the literature describing effective sexuality education and health education curricula. (For more detailed information, see Association for Sexuality Education and Training, n.d.; Cassidy, 1990; English, Sancho,

Lloyd-Kolkin and Hunter, 1990; Kirby, 1993; National Guidelines Task Force, 1991; Neutens, Drolet, Dushaw and Jubb, 1991; Rogers, Howard-Pitney and Bruce, 1990.)

The authors again worked in pairs, using the Worksheet for Evaluation of Sexuality Education Curricula, to evaluate the sexuality education curricula in the categories delineated below. Curriculum reviewers at appropriate grade levels also evaluated the selected curricula using the same criteria. Final ratings were made after an open discussion of curriculum attributes and curriculum reviewer input. (A copy of the evaluation worksheet can be found in Appendix A.)

The following categories were rated for each sexuality education curriculum:

- Comprehensiveness (Breadth)
- Comprehensiveness (Depth)
- Content Accuracy/Currency
- Skill-Building Variety (Breadth)
- Skill-Building Variety (Depth)
- Methods Variety
- Developmental Appropriateness
- Cultural Sensitivity
- Ease of Implementation
- Evaluation
- Appearance/Production Quality
- Overall Quality

Curriculum Reviewers

Critical to the review process was the examination and evaluation of the selected sexuality-education curricula by consumers, i.e., classroom teachers, health educators, resource teachers and special education teachers. Using the Worksheet for Evaluation of Sexuality Education Curricula (See Appendix A), each curriculum was evaluated by a minimum of four reviewers with experience at the appropriate grade level. Input from curriculum reviewers was incorporated in the final Evaluation of Curricula matrix. (A list of the names, addresses, certification, and years of experience of each curriculum reviewer appears in the acknowledgments section.)

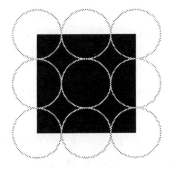

How to Use
The Consumer's Guide

The Consumer's Guide is divided into four levels as defined by the Sex Information and Education Council of the United States National Guidelines Task Force in *Guidelines for Comprehensive Sexuality Education* (1991). These levels reflect four stages of development:

- **Level 1** refers to middle childhood; ages 5 through 8; early elementary school.
- **Level 2** refers to preadolescence; ages 9 through 12; upper elementary school.
- **Level 3** refers to early adolescence; ages 12 through 15; middle school and junior high school.
- **Level 4** refers to adolescence; ages 15 through 18; high school.

An additional section describes sexuality education curricula developed for special education students.

At the beginning of each section, brief descriptions of each published school-based sexuality education curriculum present information about the curriculum title, author, year developed, latest revision, target grade level, length, curriculum description, package contents and publisher information.

Following curriculum descriptions at each level are summary matrixes. The first two matrixes, **Attributes of Curricula**, identify curriculum content, underlying philosophies, the skill-building strategies used, and the teaching strategies used. The **Evaluation of Curricula** matrix presents the reviewers' ratings of curricula based on the evaluation criteria.

The Consumer's Guide information can be used in several ways:

- If a school district is planning a curriculum adoption, but is unaware of published sexuality education curricula, program planners can read the curriculum descriptions at each level to get a better understanding of what is available.

- If a school district is looking for a sexuality education curriculum with specific attributes (e.g., a pregnancy prevention curriculum with a strong focus on skill-building strategies for middle school students), the program coordinator or teacher initially can review the **Attributes of Curricula** matrixes for **Level 3** to identify curricula that meet district needs. Then he or she can review the **Evaluation of Curricula** matrix to determine how that specific curriculum was rated by sexuality educators, curriculum specialists and classroom teachers. Finally, the reviewer can consult the program description for information about where to order the curriculum.

- If program coordinators or teachers are looking for a more comprehensive sexuality education curriculum for high school students, they can review the **Evaluation of Curricula** matrix for **Level 4** to identify curricula with high ratings on comprehensiveness. Then they can refer to the **Attributes of Curricula** matrixes and specific curriculum descriptions to get more information about the attributes of selected curricula.

- Finally, using the blank matrixes and the worksheet in Appendix A, a school district can evaluate their existing sexuality curriculum to identify curriculum attributes and evaluate the comprehensiveness, cultural sensitivity, ease of implementation, etc., of the adopted or district-developed curriculum. Subsequently, the district curriculum can be enhanced to include missing attributes.

Elementary Curricula
Levels
1 & 2

Learning About Family Life

Title: *Learning About Family Life:*
Resources for Learning and Teaching
Author: Barbara Sprung
Year Developed 1992
Latest Revision: None
Target Grade Level: Kindergarten through Grade 3
Length: 43 stories
Cost: $250.00

Curriculum Description

Curriculum Focus

Sexuality is part of daily life, and foundations in sexuality education should begin at an early age. The curriculum supports the concept that sex is pleasurable and that curiosity about one's body is natural and healthy. Every aspect of human experience that children encounter in their daily lives can be discussed, provided it is presented in a developmentally appropriate manner. The curriculum for early primary grades is based on four elements:

- interpersonal relationships
- human growth, development, sexuality and reproduction
- responsible personal behavior
- building strong families

Lesson Format

Each of the 43 lessons includes:

- A short story about a family life issue.
- Suggestions for leading classroom discussion with sample questions.
- Activities—grouped by grades K–1 and 2–3.
- Comments and Considerations—providing additional background information.
- Resources—additional books dealing with the issues discussed in the lesson.

Learning About Family Life (continued)

Package Contents

The package contains three components:
- Learning about Family Life: The Big Book—illustrated stories about family life issues and a chart identifying grade appropriateness of each story.
- Learning about Family Life: Resources—discussion guidelines and extended activities for Grades K–1 and 2–3.
- Family, Friends, and Feelings—a journal in which students record their thoughts and feelings.

Resources of supporting organizations and a listing of adult background readings are included. A list of publishers and materials appears at the back of the book.

Publisher Information

Bantam, Doubleday, Bell Publishing Group, The Education and Library Division, 1540 Broadway, New York, New York 10036; (800) 223-6834.

F.L.A.S.H. 5/6

Title: *F.L.A.S.H. (Family Life and Sexual Health) 5/6*
Authors: Elizabeth Reiss, MS, and Pamela Hillard
Year Developed: 1985
Latest Revision: 1988
Target Grade Level: Grades 5 and 6
Length: 15 lessons
Cost: $25.00

Curriculum Description

Curriculum Focus

The curriculum is based on "universal" values which are outlined specifically:

- Respect must be given for the individuality of the student and his or her peers in the classroom.
- Honest communication is fundamental in all relationships.
- People have a responsibility to learn as much as possible about themselves and others.

The goal is to enable individuals to become knowledgeable about human development and reproduction and to respect themselves, their families and all persons.

Lesson Format

This curriculum addresses nine main topic areas within 15 lesson plans. Sequential order of presentation is not essential. Each lesson includes:

- Student learning objectives.
- Materials needed for the lesson.
- An agenda.
- An activity.
- Related activities for integrated learning—suggestions for integrating content and activities in other areas (e.g., social studies, math, language arts).
- Homework—Activities centering on getting parents or other adults actively involved.

Package Contents

Worksheets and transparency masters are included. Supplemental materials for the teacher include a special presentation section with specific tips on how to plan units and how to prepare administrators and parents. A section on how to direct small groups and guest speakers and how to use worksheets and question boxes is included. An appendix contains sample parent letters, state guidelines and regulations, a glossary, local resources, available video materials and information on recognizing and reporting sexual abuse.

Publisher Information

Seattle–King County Department of Public Health, Family Planning Publications, 2124 4th Avenue, Seattle, Washington 98121; (206) 296-4672.

Growing Up

Title: *Growing Up and Learning to Feel Good About Yourself: An Educator's Bilingual Guide to Teaching Puberty*

Authors: Barbara Petrich-Kelly and Kristen Rohm
Year Developed: 1992
Latest Revision: None
Target Grade Level: Grades 5 and 6
Length: 8 lessons
Cost: $29.95

Curriculum Description

Curriculum Focus

This English/Spanish curriculum provides accurate information about functions of the male and female reproductive systems, common puberty dilemmas and problem-solving strategies. These topics are covered in three general areas: self-awareness, self-protection and self-appreciation/self-esteem. The curriculum encourages young children to feel normal and natural about their sexuality.

Lesson Format

The curriculum follows this format for each lesson:

- Purpose.
- Materials.
- Concepts and Methods—Key concepts are listed in the left-hand column across from the methods, along with the approximate time for that portion of the lesson. Methods to achieve each key concept include introduction, review, activities, wrap-up and homework.
- Notes—Teaching tips are blocked within the methods section to highlight certain aspects of an activity.
- Homework—Assignments, reminders and praise are given, along with reminders to the teacher about materials for the next lesson.

Growing Up *(continued)*

Package Contents

- English and Spanish versions of the teacher's guide.
- A Teacher Resource section (including student worksheets) providing background information about importance of sexuality education, puberty, male/female anatomy, answering student questions, masturbation, homosexuality and bisexuality.
- Evaluation of the curriculum pilot study.
- Resource list of books, videos and pamphlets.

Publisher Information

Planned Parenthood of Santa Barbara, Ventura, and San Luis Obispo Counties, Inc., 518 Garden Street, Santa Barbara, California 93101; (805) 963-2445.

P.S.I. (Preteens)

Title: *Postponing Sexual Involvement:*
An Educational Series for Preteens
Authors: Marion Howard and Marie Mitchell
Year Developed: 1990
Latest Revision: None
Target Grade Level: Grades 5 and 6
Length: Four lessons, plus one reinforcement lesson to
be conducted three months after the fourth
lesson.
Cost: $80.00

Curriculum Description

Curriculum Focus

This curriculum was developed to help preteens learn the skills of resisting pressure to become sexually involved before they are ready for such involvement.

The emphasis for this curriculum is threefold:
- Help preteens understand natural curiosity about sex.
- Increase the ability of preteens to secure information and advice in healthy ways.
- Assist preteens in coping with social and peer pressures by developing the skills to say "no" to behaviors in which they do not wish to engage.

Five sessions present information and activities related to (1) societal pressures to becoming sexually active, (2) risks of early sexual behavior, (3) peer pressure, (4) assertiveness techniques and (5) reinforcement in using new skills.

Lesson Format

The format for each lesson is presented as follows:
- Time.
- Supplies.
- Number in group.
- Seating—The arrangement of desks in the classroom is suggested for each lesson.

- Purpose of the lesson.
- Concepts.
- Lesson segments—For each concept within the lesson, authors give the purpose of the lesson, the approximate time needed, specific instructions in how to teach the activity, a scripted lecture from the videocassette, questions for discussion, a summary or closing and sample responses to the activity.
- Handouts—The authors provide a "Pressure Lines" handout in Lesson III and "Situations" handouts in Lesson IV.

Package Contents

- Educator's Guide—Includes all lessons and student worksheets.
- Videocassette to be used in conjunction with the Educator's Guide.

Publisher Information

Emory/Grady Teen Services Program, Grady Memorial Hospital, 80 Butler Street, Atlanta, Georgia 30335-1801; (404) 616-3513.

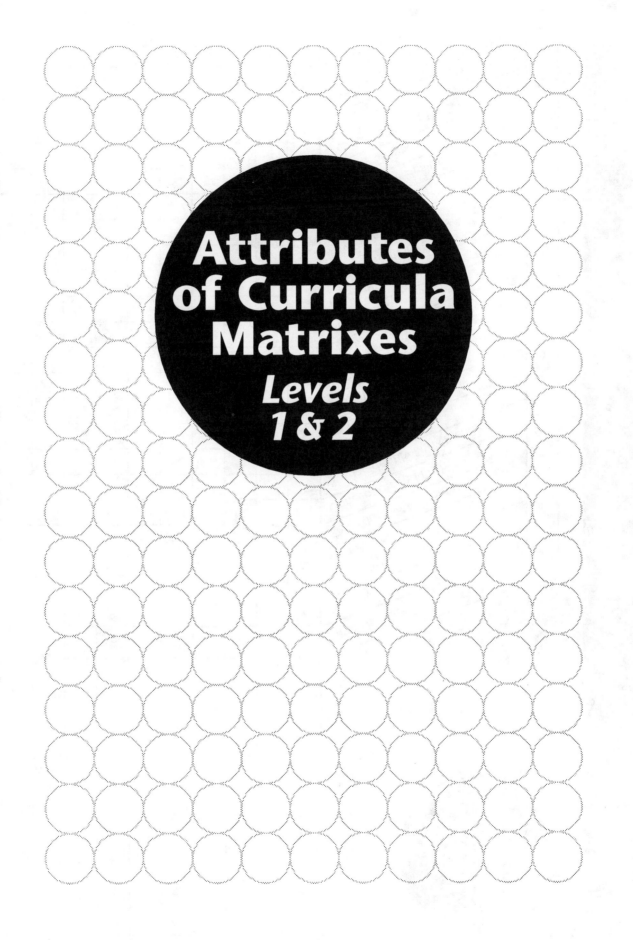

Attributes
of Curricula
Matrixes
Levels
1 & 2

Attributes of Curricula

Levels 1 & 2

Curriculum	Abstinence	Using Protection if Sexually Active	Philosophy Not Clear	Responsibility for Decisions	Healthy Sexuality	Reproductive Health	Sexual Exploitation	HIV Prevention	STD Prevention	Pregnancy Prevention	Abstinence	HIV Transmission	STD Transmission	Sexual Expression	Parenting	Relationships	Sexual Identity and Orientation	Conception and Birth	Reproductive Anatomy/Physiology	Gender Roles	Body Image	Puberty	Page Number
	Philosophy			**Content**																			
Learning About Family Life (Level 1)	*					✓	✓	✓	*	*	*	*	✓		✓	✓	✓	✓	✓	✓	✓	✓	13
F.L.A.S.H. 5/6 (Level 2)		✓					✓	✓					✓				✓		✓	✓			15
Growing Up (Level 2)						✓		✓	✓	✓			✓				✓			✓			17
P.S.I. (Preteens) (Level 2)				✓				✓				✓			✓		✓				✓		19

* Not appropriate for this age group.

(For descriptions of attributes, see p. 25.)

Curriculum

Levels 1 & 2 (continued)

Curriculum	Parent/Guardian Involvement	Peer Helper Component	Community Speakers/Involvement	Audiovisual Materials	Skills Practice and Rehearsal	Case Studies/Scenarios	Cooperative Learning/Small Groups	Journals/Story Writing	Student Worksheets	Large-Group Discussion	Teacher Lecture	Anonymous Question Box	Groundrules	Planning/Goal-Setting Skills	Decision-Making Skills	Conflict-Management Skills	Refusal Skills	Assertiveness Skills	General Communication Skills	Community Resources	Perceived STD/HIV Risk	Perceived Pregnancy Risk	Peer Norms	Consequences of Decisions	Influences on Decisions	Self-Awareness/Self-Esteem	Personal Values
Learning About Family Life				✓	✓	✓	✓	✓	✓		✓	✓			✓	✓	✓		✓	✓	✓				✓		✓
F.L.A.S.H. 5/6		✓			✓	✓	✓			✓	✓	✓	✓	✓	✓					✓					✓	✓	✓
Growing Up		✓			✓	✓	✓			✓	✓	✓	✓		✓					✓					✓		
P.S.I. (Preteens)					✓	✓	✓	✓			✓	✓	✓	✓				✓			✓					✓	

Teaching Strategies | **Skill-Building Strategies**

23

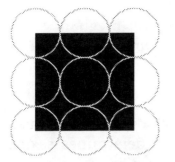

Descriptions of Attributes

Content

Puberty
Physical changes that occur in males and females during puberty; individual differences in growth rates; feelings/emotions associated with changes during puberty.

Body Image
Individual variations in size, shape, etc.; uniqueness of each person; physical appearance as determined by heredity, environment, and health habits; disabilities; portrayal of body image by media; effect of physical appearance on how people interact with others.

Gender Roles
Messages from families, friends, media and society about how males and females should behave; both genders having similar talents, characteristics, strengths, hopes and need for equal opportunities; gender role stereotypes; laws protecting the rights of men and women.

Reproductive Anatomy/Physiology
Human body has capability to reproduce; body parts have correct names and specific functions; maturation of reproductive organs occurs at puberty; hormones influence sexual and reproductive function.

Conception and Birth

Union of sperm and egg in fertilization; heredity; pregnancy and development of the fetus; genetic disorders and birth defects; stages of birth; medical procedures and new reproductive technology.

Sexual Identity and Orientation

Attraction; definition of sexual orientation, including heterosexual, homosexual and bisexual; theories about what determines sexual orientation; mistreatment and denial of rights based on sexual orientation; support services for questioning youth.

Relationships

Definition of family; types of families; roles and responsibilities of family members; friendships with people of both genders; expressing love and affection; dating; importance of honest and open communication; shared responsibility in marriage; divorce; community resources.

Parenting

Skills and information needed to make good parents; balance of parenting and full-time job; difficulties of being a teen parent; different types of parenting as children get older; raising a child with special needs.

Sexual Expression

Ways to show love and affection without having sex; natural physical response to touch; sexual response experienced differently by each person; masturbation, fantasy and shared sexual behavior; capacity to respond sexually throughout life.

STD Transmission

Causes of sexually transmitted disease; modes of transmission; signs and symptoms; long-term effects of untreated STD; importance of open communication with partner; community resources for testing, treatment and counseling; hotlines.

HIV Transmission

Type of sexually transmitted disease; caused by human immunodeficiency virus (HIV); modes of transmission; signs and symptoms; differences from other STD; community resources for testing, treatment and counseling; hotlines.

Abstinence

Safest, most effective method of preventing STD, HIV infection and pregnancy; advantages of choosing not to have sex; physical and emotional readiness for sexual intercourse; importance of open and honest communication; always having a choice; giving and receiving pleasure without having sex.

Pregnancy Prevention

Decisions to have children based on religious beliefs, personal values and cultural traditions; methods of contraception, including advantages, disadvantages and effective use; individual responsibility for getting and using protection; importance of honest and open communication with partner.

STD Prevention

Methods of STD prevention, including advantages, disadvantages and effective use; individual responsibility for getting and using protection; importance of honest and open communication with partner; community resources.

HIV Prevention

Methods of HIV infection prevention, including advantages, disadvantages and effective use; individual responsibility for getting and using protection; importance of honest and open communication with partner; community resources.

Sexual Exploitation

Sexual harassment; sexual abuse; acquaintance rape; other types of sexual exploitation; individual rights related to any type of sexual exploitation; protecting oneself, including avoiding potentially dangerous situations and learning self-defense; community resources; support services.

Reproductive Health

Individual responsibility for health; importance of cleanliness, nutrition and exercise; routine physical examination; breast self-examination; testicular self-examination; prenatal effects of smoking, drinking and using other substances; birth defects and genetic counseling.

Philosophy

Promotes Healthy Sexuality

The curriculum presents sexuality as a natural and healthy part of everyday living. It is maintained that each person expresses his or her sexuality in a variety of ways based on personal background and experience. The curriculum addresses the physical, psychological, emotional, social, ethical and spiritual dimensions of healthy sexuality.

Promotes Responsibility for Decisions

The curriculum supports each individual's right and obligation to make decisions about his or her sexuality. The curriculum empowers young people to make responsible decisions by helping them examine internal and external influences on personal decisions, recognize short- and long-term consequences of their decisions for themselves and others, and access information and services through personal support systems and community resources.

Promotes Abstinence

The curriculum presents abstinence as the safest, most effective way to prevent sexually transmitted disease, HIV infection and pregnancy. It addresses the advantages of choosing not to have sexual intercourse, the benefits of delaying sex, and the risks of having sex if a person is not ready or does not want to.

Promotes Using Protection If Sexually Active

The curriculum acknowledges that some young people will have sexual intercourse and presents methods of protection from sexually transmitted disease, HIV infection and pregnancy. It discusses advantages, disadvantages and effectiveness of these methods.

Philosophy Not Clear

The curriculum has no clear focus.

Skill-Building Strategies

Examining Personal Values

The curriculum includes activities that help young people identify what they believe, what they think is important, and how personal values affect their sexuality-related decisions.

Increasing Self-Awareness/Building Self-Esteem

The curriculum includes activities that help young people become aware of their likes and dislikes, capabilities and limitations, talents and skills; appreciate their own uniqueness; and accept individual differences.

Examining Influences on Decisions

The curriculum includes activities that focus on the internal influences (wanting to be accepted, be part of a group, take risks, feel normal, feel good, etc.) and external influences (parents/caregivers, other adults, peers, media) that affect sexuality-related decisions.

Identifying Consequences of Decisions

The curriculum includes activities that help young people look at short- and long-term physical, emotional, social and legal consequences of sexuality-related decisions for themselves and others.

Addressing Peer Norms

The curriculum includes activities that allow young people to share their perceptions of norms related to abstinence and use of protection, and that promote changes in the normative message (e.g., making posters and pamphlets to support the message that "not everyone is doing it").

Examining Perceived Pregnancy Risk

The curriculum includes activities to help young people examine the risk of getting pregnant (based on specific behaviors) and understand how they can change their behaviors to decrease the probability of pregnancy.

Examining Perceived STD/HIV Risk

The curriculum includes activities to help young people examine the risk of getting a sexually transmitted disease, including HIV, and understand how they can change their behaviors to reduce the risk of becoming infected with STD/HIV.

29

Accessing Community Resources

The curriculum includes activities that help young people identify sources of information and services in the community, including community agencies, hotlines, clinics and support groups.

Building General Communication Skills

The curriculum includes activities where young people learn to communicate clearly—verbally and nonverbally; to listen actively; and to express their thoughts, feelings, attitudes, beliefs, values and ideas about sexuality-related issues.

Building Assertiveness Skills

The curriculum includes activities that give young people practice in saying what they think and standing up for what they believe, without hurting or denying the rights of others. It also helps students understand the differences between passive, assertive and aggressive responses.

Building Refusal Skills

The curriculum includes activities that help young people practice effective ways to say "no" without jeopardizing their peer and family relationships.

Building Conflict-Management Skills

The curriculum includes activities that help young people solve problems and resolve conflicts in relationships without using guilt, anger and/or intimidation. It also provides opportunities to practice negotiation skills.

Building Decision-Making Skills

The curriculum includes activities that help young people examine real-life situations, generate possible solutions, and anticipate the short- and long-term consequences of having sex and having unprotected sex, as well as understand how each decision can affect subsequent decisions.

Building Planning/Goal-Setting Skills

The curriculum includes activities that help young people examine personal expectations and those of others, identify short- and long-term personal goals, and identify barriers to achieving their personal goals. It also provides opportunities to use planning skills in situations related to having sex or having unprotected sex.

Teaching Strategies

Groundrules
With student input, the teacher establishes groundrules for class-room discussion of sexuality-related issues.

Anonymous Question Box
An anonymous question box is set up so that students can ask questions or express feelings and concerns without fear of embar-rassment.

Teacher Lecture
The teacher provides key information directly to students with a minimum of class participation and interruption.

Large-Group Discussion
In an open discussion involving the entire class, students are guided by the teacher to share ideas, thoughts and beliefs about a sexuality-related issue.

Student Worksheets
A variety of written questions or forms are used to help students focus on particular topics. This strategy allows the sharing of opin-ions and ideas without having to discuss them openly with the rest of the class.

Journals/Story Writing
Students are given opportunities to write their thoughts and feelings about the sexuality-related issues discussed in class in personal jour-nals or diaries.

Cooperative Learning/Small Groups
Lessons include small-group discussions about sexuality-related issues. Students are assigned certain roles and responsibilities within the group.

Case Studies/Scenarios
Lessons include case studies and real-life scenarios to help students practice personal and social skills.

Skills Practice and Rehearsal

Students are given a variety of opportunities to practice newly learned personal and social skills, including roleplays, small-group activities and worksheets.

Audiovisual Materials

The teacher uses audiovisual materials when presenting information and/or skills (transparencies, videos, slides, films, etc.).

Community Speakers/Involvement

Outside speakers from community agencies are asked to present sexuality-related information or skills.

Peer Helper Component

Same-age or cross-age peers are used in the presentation of sexuality-related information or skills.

Parent/Guardian Involvement

Homework assignments and curriculum activities are designed to be completed by parents or caregivers and their children.

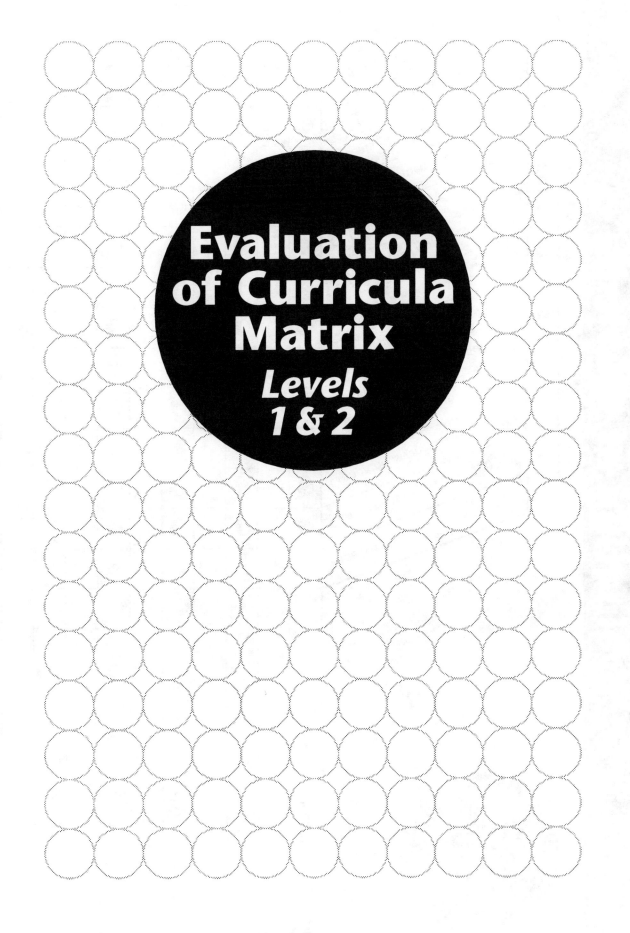

Evaluation of Curricula Matrix
Levels 1 & 2

Evaluation of Curricula

Levels 1 & 2

Evaluation Criteria

Curriculum

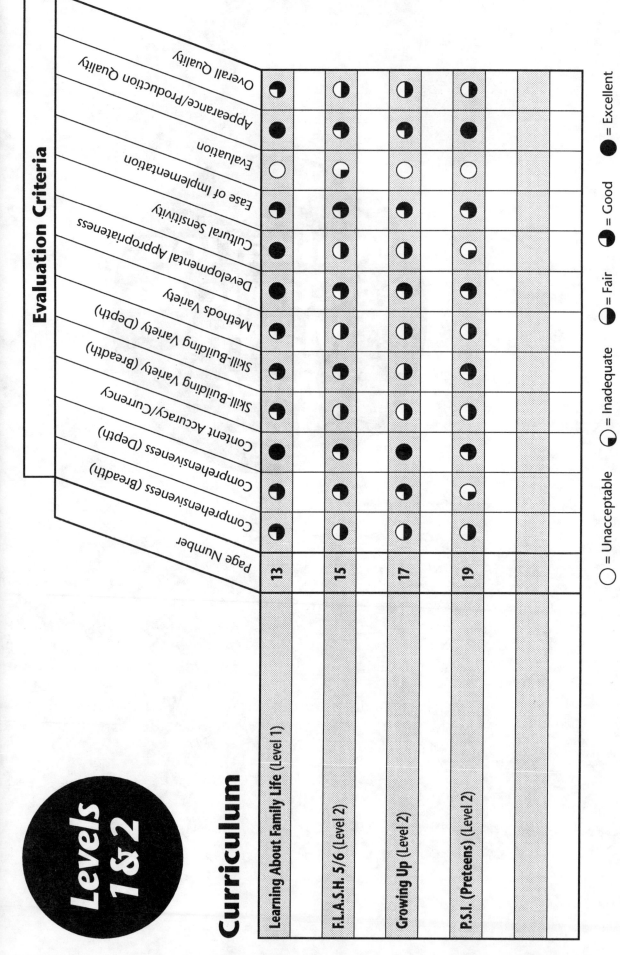

Curriculum	Page Number
Learning About Family Life (Level 1)	13
F.L.A.S.H. 5/6 (Level 2)	15
Growing Up (Level 2)	17
P.S.I. (Preteens) (Level 2)	19

Evaluation criteria (columns): Comprehensiveness (Breadth), Comprehensiveness (Depth), Content Accuracy/Currency, Skill-Building Variety (Breadth), Skill-Building Variety (Depth), Methods Variety, Developmental Appropriateness, Cultural Sensitivity, Ease of Implementation, Evaluation, Appearance/Production Quality, Overall Quality

Legend:
- ○ = Unacceptable
- ◔ = Inadequate
- ◑ = Fair
- ◕ = Good
- ● = Excellent

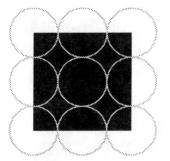

Descriptions of Evaluation Criteria

Evaluation Criteria

Comprehensiveness (Breadth)

The curriculum includes *all* developmentally appropriate key concepts as described by the *Guidelines for Comprehensive Sexuality Education* (National Guidelines Task Force, 1991).

Comprehensiveness (Depth)

The curriculum includes *all* subconcepts and developmental messages within each key concept as described by the *Guidelines for Comprehensive Sexuality Education* (National Guidelines Task Force, 1991).

Content Accuracy/Currency

The curriculum provides accurate information about sexuality-related topics and is based on current research and theory. Graphs, charts and tables are current and representative of the target population.

The curriculum is up to date and presents information in ways that interest today's young people. Graphs, charts, language and pictures reflect current issues and trends.

Skill-Building Variety (Breadth)
The curriculum provides activities to build a variety of personal and social skills: decision-making, general communication, assertiveness, refusal, conflict management and planning/goal-setting skills.

Skill-Building Variety (Depth)
The curriculum addresses each personal and social skill comprehensively: the skill is introduced focusing on its importance; steps for skill development are presented; the skill is modeled for students; the skill is practiced and rehearsed with a variety of situations; and feedback/reinforcement is provided.

Methods Variety
To meet the diverse needs and learning styles of students, the curriculum provides a variety of instructional strategies for providing key information; encouraging creative expression; sharing thoughts, feelings and opinions; and developing critical thinking skills.

Developmental Appropriateness
The curriculum presents sexuality-related information, instructional strategies, and personal and social skills appropriate for the cognitive, emotional and social developmental level and personal experience of the targeted grades. Lessons are adaptable to individual student needs.

Cultural Sensitivity
The curriculum does not contain information or activities that are biased in terms of race or ethnicity, sex or gender roles, family types, sexual orientation, and/or age. It portrays a variety of social groups and lifestyles in its examples, pictures and descriptions. Instructional strategies take into account the cultural and ethnic values, customs and practices of the community.

Ease of Implementation
The curriculum includes features that make it "user friendly." That is, all materials and master copies necessary for implementation are included; it is well organized, with clear, thorough instructions; it can easily be updated; and it provides references and support materials for teachers.

Evaluation

The curriculum provides methods for evaluating levels of student knowledge, attitudes and/or skills that are consistent with curriculum goals and lesson objectives.

Appearance/Production Quality

The curriculum is clearly written, up to date, aesthetically pleasing (including print quality), and likely to elicit student interest.

Overall Quality

Overall assessment of the quality of the curriculum is based on scores in comprehensiveness, content accuracy/currency, skill-building variety, methods variety, developmental appropriateness, cultural sensitivity, ease of implementation, evaluation and appearance/ production quality.

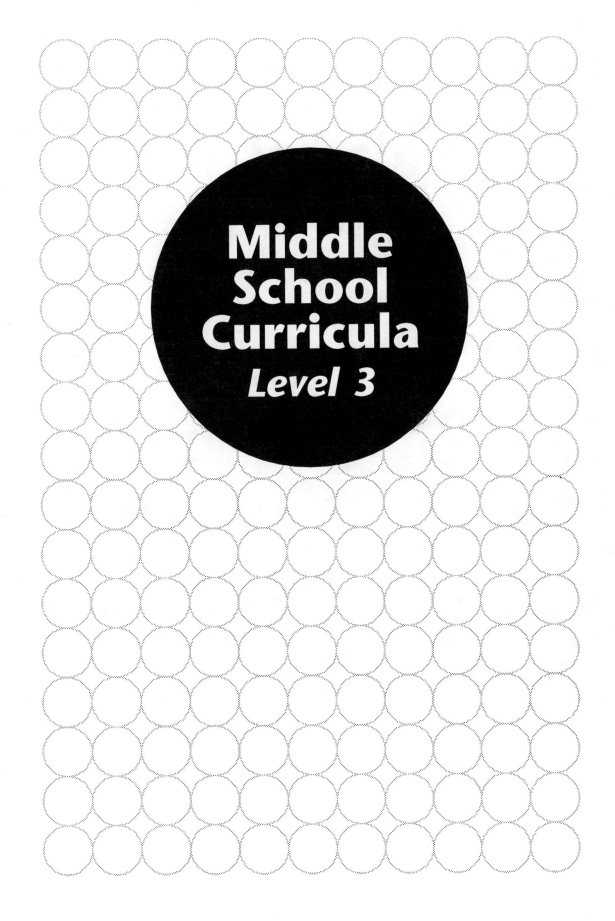

Middle
School
Curricula
Level 3

3-R

Title: *Adolescent Reproductive Risk Reduction ("3-R")*
Author: Originally developed by Lucinda Thomas, adapted by the South Carolina Department of Health and Environmental Control
Year Developed: Originally developed in 1979 by Thomas; South Carolina version began in 1989
Latest Revision: None
Target Grade Level: Grades 7 and 8
Length: 15 lessons for grade 7; 13 lessons for grade 8
Cost: No cost

Curriculum Description

Curriculum Focus

Overall goals of the "3-R" curriculum are to
- Enable teens to delay early sexual activity, thus reducing teen pregnancy rates.
- Help teens reduce risky behaviors that cause poor adolescent health and poor health of their future children.
- Increase communication skills with parents.

The "3-R" curriculum builds upon four concepts: (1) knowledge of the reproductive system, (2) health and social consequences of sexual activity, (3) ways to reduce and protect oneself from the consequences of sexual activity and (4) building relationships with respect, assertive communication and acceptance of responsibility for one's own activities. Respect, responsibility and restraint are themes within curriculum units.

Lesson Format

Each lesson adheres to the following format:
- Purpose of the class.
- Student objectives.
- Notes to the teacher—An explanation of major concepts and suggestions for promotion of particular activities is given.
- Teacher preparation—A complete list of materials needed for the lesson is included.
- Activities—A sequential list of activities to be incorporated in the lesson is provided.

Package Contents

- Complete report on the research and results of the "3-R" project study.
- The introduction to the guide includes: values promoted by "3-R," effects of "3-R" instruction, parent comments, achieving community support, dealing with opposition, parent permission, suggestions for implementation, complete teacher training materials, references, audiovisual lists for grades 7 and 8, audiovisual sources and program planning worksheets.
- The grade 7 and grade 8 curriculum packages.
- The grade 7 and grade 8 parent/child homework sheets.
- A handouts package for each curriculum.
- A complete evaluation package for each curriculum.
- "Bay City Kids", a program of trigger videos that depict sexual dilemmas, to be used for initiating guided class discussion.

Publisher Information

South Carolina Department of Health and Environmental Control, Division of Children's Health, Robert Mills Complex, P.O. Box 101106, Columbia, South Carolina 29211; (803) 737-4061.

Family Life

Title: *Family Life Sexuality Education Program*
Authors: Six Rivers Planned Parenthood
Year Developed: 1977
Latest Revision: 1991
Target Grade Level: Grades 5 through 9
Length: Sixteen-day course outline: three-day grade 6 outline, five-day grade 7 outline and an eight-day grade 8 outline. There are three combined class lessons and numerous optional lessons.
Cost: $35.00

Curriculum Description

Curriculum Focus

The curriculum is designed to help young people deal positively with the emotional, social and physical changes experienced at puberty. It is tailored to help them express their emerging sexuality in positive ways. Responsible decision-making is the major focus of the curriculum. A goal of the curriculum is to foster increased communication between parents and children about sexuality.

Lesson Format

A course outline of lesson topics is included in the introduction. General objectives and an overview of each unit precede the sublessons. Each sublesson includes:

- A stated purpose.
- The length of time the lesson takes.
- A list of materials needed.
- An outline of procedures.
- Suggested discussion questions, along with needed reproductive handout masters.
- Suggested video presentations with accompanying sublessons for class presentation.

43

Family Life *(continued)*

Package Contents

In addition to the core unit lessons, an evaluation section includes a post-test, student course evaluation forms, state education code of standards, and parent consent forms. There is also a parent/child communication supplement that includes a letter of introduction to parents and activities to help students initiate discussion with parents. A supplemental guide offers suggestions for activities that expand concepts presented in the core curriculum. Supplemental activities include the use of newspapers, videos, diagrams and charts which can be used in pre-lesson introductory activities or as follow-up reinforcement activities.

Publisher Information

Six Rivers Planned Parenthood, 2316 Harrison Avenue, Eureka, California 95501; (707) 442-2961.

F.L.A.S.H. 7/8

Title: *F.L.A.S.H. (Family Life and Sexual Health) 7/8*
Authors: Elizabeth Reiss, MS, and Pamela Hillard
Year Developed: 1986
Latest Revision: 1988
Target Grade Level: Grades 7 and 8
Length: 25 lessons
Cost: $40.00

Curriculum Description

Curriculum Focus

The curriculum is based on "universal" values which are outlined specifically:

- Respect must be given for the individuality of the student and his or her peers in the classroom.
- Honest communication is fundamental in all relationships.
- People have a responsibility to learn as much as possible about themselves and others.

Its goal is to enable individuals to become knowledgeable about human development and reproduction and to respect themselves and others.

Lesson Format

An overview section gives each lesson title and a summary of objectives for the lesson. The curriculum is designed to be integrated with other academic areas and does not have to be taught in sequence. For example, it is suggested that the lessons on STD be included in a unit with other contagious diseases. The five lessons on communication might be scheduled at the end of the semester, when the class has had time to build rapport. The curriculum is mostly self-contained. Each lesson is outlined as follows:

- Student learning objectives.
- Materials needed.
- Time needed to complete each lesson.
- Agenda and activities.

Package Contents

Worksheets, transparency masters and student reference sheets supplement each lesson. Evaluation and reinforcement of student knowledge is included in competitive game format. *The Sexuality Educator* pretest and posttest is designed to help prepare teachers in content knowledge and alert them to noted areas of weakness. A list of suggested texts that teachers can use to improve background knowledge is provided and suggestions for working with administrators and parents are included. Sample parent letters, family homework letters, sample letters for resource people, state regulations, community resources, video resources, guidelines for recognizing sexual abuse and an overview of F.L.A.S.H. 5/6 are also included. The package contains 70 student handouts and 26 transparency masters.

Publisher Information

Seattle–King County Department of Public Health, Family Planning Publications, 2124 4th Avenue, Seattle, Washington 98121; (206) 296-4672.

Healthy Sexuality

Title: *Healthy Sexuality*—A Teaching Module
for Middle Schools
Authors: Kay Nation and Louise Miller
Year Developed: 1992
Latest Revision: None
Target Grade Level: Middle School, ages 12 to 14
Length: 10 lessons, 12 to 15 class periods
Cost: See note below.

Curriculum Description

Curriculum Focus

Healthy Sexuality combines social support and a skills-based approach to sex education. These two approaches teach skills to build self-efficacy and empower students through a social support system they build for themselves. These skills are built in the classroom and reinforced at home. This curriculum assumes that the area of puberty has already been discussed, as this is part of a comprehensive school health education program.

Healthy Sexuality teaches "Personal Power" skills throughout the curriculum. Skills include:
- Protect myself and others.
- Own my responsibilities.
- Wait, stop and think.
- Express myself clearly.
- Respect myself and others.

Fourteen value statements for the curriculum indicate that healthy sexuality is natural, holistic and never coercive, and that abstaining from intercourse promotes responsibility and prevents disease.

Lesson Format

Each lesson in the curriculum includes the following items:
- Learning objectives.
- Summary of activities—List of lesson activities and the approximate completion time.
- Points to ponder.

- Preparation—Information that should be reviewed by the instructor prior to the lesson.
- Materials needed—Specifies quantities needed for a class of 25–30 students.
- Introduction.
- Activities—Each activity is presented in detail and in order of use in the lesson.
- Wrap-up—Closure to the lesson includes summary, review, homework and praise.

Package Contents

- Curriculum Guide contains curriculum overview, lessons, handouts and student worksheets.
- Two videos: "Saying No...A Few Words to Young Adults About Sex" (18 minutes) and "Flashback: An AIDS Video Drama for Teens" (13 minutes).

Publisher Information

Rocky Mountain Center for Health Promotion and Education, 7525 West 10th Avenue, Lakewood, Colorado 80215-5141; (303) 239-6494.

Note: To adopt the curriculum, a school district must send a team of six to ten professionals from the school district for training. The team should be comprised of an administrator, a school nurse, a parent, and teachers. The cost of the three-day training and three manuals for the team is $1000.00. After the initial three-day team training, the cost for an individual teacher to train is $160.00.

Values and Choices

Title: *Human Sexuality: Values and Choices,* A Value-Based Curriculum for 7th and 8th Grade, Revised Edition.

Authors: John Forliti, Lucy Kapp, Sandy Naughton, Lynn Young; Revising Editor: Dorothy L. Williams

Year Developed: 1986
Latest Revision: 1991
Target Grade Level: Grades 7 and 8
Length: 15 lessons
Cost: $450.00

Curriculum Description

Curriculum Focus

The curriculum focuses on seven values essential for maintaining positive human relationships anywhere in our culture: equality, self-control, promise-keeping, responsibility, respect, honesty and social justice. Emphasis is placed on parents/guardians as co-educators, through activities that encourage communication at home. The curriculum includes abstinence messages throughout the 15 lessons. The curriculum does include a lesson on birth control as the second-best alternative to abstinence.

Lesson Format

Each lesson is presented in the following format:
- An introductory paragraph to the lesson.
- Goals.
- Values emphasized—The authors indicate which of the seven values will be emphasized in the lesson.
- Concept.
- Attitudes.
- Behaviors.
- Knowledge.
- Key vocabulary.
- Teacher preparation checklist.
- Learning activities—The introduction, review, activities and closure segments of the lesson are scripted along with the time needed to accomplish each of them.
- Teacher reference—Suggested answers to typical student questions, activity sheets and homework assignments.

Values and Choices (continued)

Package Contents

Essential Components include a Teachers' Manual, videotape and Guide for Parents of Adolescents. Optional Components include the Reinforcement and Review Activity book, the "My Values, My Choices" student thought book, the teacher's guide to "My Values, My Choices," a values poster and values cards.

Publisher Information

Search Institute of Minneapolis, Thresher Square West, 700 South Third Street, Suite 210, Minneapolis, Minnesota 55415; (800) 888-7828.

Into Adolescence

Titles:
1. *A Time of Change*
2. *Choosing Abstinence*
3. *Learning About Reproduction and Birth*
4. *Learning About HIV*

Authors:
1. Catherine S. Golliher
2. Dale Zevin
3. Catherine S. Golliher
4. Jory Post and Carole McPherson

Year Developed: 1989

Latest Revision: 1, 2 and 3. None
4. 1993

Target Grade Level: Grades 5 through 8

Length:
1. 6 lessons
2. 7 lessons
3. 6 lessons
4. 12 lessons

Cost: $23.50 per module

Curriculum Description

Curriculum Focus

The modules listed here are those in the *Into Adolescence* component of the Contemporary Health Series that deal with sexuality. *A Time of Change* clears up misconceptions and concerns students have regarding changes in their own bodies. *Choosing Abstinence* focuses on promoting responsible personal behavior and the idea that sexual activity is inappropriate for middle school students. *Learning About Reproduction and Birth* explains every aspect of reproduction and birth that middle school students want to know. *Learning About HIV* provides students with open and honest information related to knowledge and awareness of HIV/AIDS. Additional related content and skills are taught in other modules in the series.

Lesson Format

Each lesson is presented as follows:
- Objectives.
- Time.
- Overview.

- Instructional strategies.
- Teacher materials and preparation.
- Procedure.
- Evaluation.
- Homework and follow-up activities.
- Alternative strategies for advanced students—Activities are presented for advanced students in the form of cooperative learning, guided discovery and independent study.
- Student worksheets.
- Teacher keys—The teacher key has completed answers from the student worksheet assignments.
- Teacher background information—Detailed information for specific lessons is provided; for example, extensive information for teachers is given for the Anatomy and Physiology lesson.
- Diagrams—Drawings are provided for lessons on anatomy and physiology.

Package Contents

Each module provides background information about a specific aspect of sexuality; groundrules and realistic expectations; a list of the lessons and their related objectives; a glossary of terms and definitions; and a student workbook.

Publisher Information

ETR Associates, P.O. Box 1830, Santa Cruz, California 95061-1830; (800) 321-4407.

Life Planning

Title: *Life Planning Education: A Youth Development Program*
Author: The Center for Population Options
Year Developed: 1985
Latest Revision: 1989
Target Grade Level: Grades 7 through 9
Length: 10 chapters
Cost: $44.95

Curriculum Description

Curriculum Focus

The philosophy behind this curriculum is that young people can make good choices and decisions if they have sufficient information about the possible consequences, as well as knowledge of available resources. The focus is on assisting teens in planning for their future vocational and family life so they can achieve their full potential in both areas.

Lesson Format

The curriculum consists of three units; the first two units contain three chapters and the final unit contains four chapters. The format is as follows:

- Purpose.
- Materials.
- Time—The time required for each lesson is stated in each chapter.
- Procedure—The procedure to be followed is stated in a step-by-step process.
- Discussion points—This section has potential questions for student response.
- Planning notes—Some activities include planning notes when preparations must be made before the instructor begins to conduct the activity.

Life Planning *(continued)*

Package Contents

- Preliminaries—A special section for the leader that includes "how-to's," teaching techniques and strategies for program implementation.
- Life planning education activities—Experiential activities designed to actively involve teens in the learning process.
- Resources—Recommended resources related to all aspects of life planning education.
- Appendixes—Supplementary information for the leader is included.
- Life planning education in Hispanic communities—This guide (located at the end of the curriculum) was developed for leaders working with Hispanic teens.

Publisher Information

Center for Population Options, 1025 Vermont Avenue, Suite 210, Washington, D.C. 20005; (202) 347-5700.

Living Smart (Middle School)

Title: *Living Smart: Understanding Sexuality in the Teen Years*
Authors: Pennie Core-Gebhart, Susan J. Hart
and Michael Young
Year Developed: 1991
Latest Revision: 1994 (Retitled *Sex Can Wait: An Abstinence-Based Sexuality Curriculum for Middle School*)
Target Grade Level: Grades 7 and 8
Length: 24 lessons
Cost: $59.95

Curriculum Description

Curriculum Focus

The curriculum is designed to promote abstinence as the most viable option in sexual decision making. It is important for adolescents to acquire skills necessary for emotional growth and maturation before making a commitment to a sexual relationship.

Lesson Format

Each lesson is presented as follows:
- Teaching objectives.
- Instructor background—Information on the topic for each lesson is provided for the instructor.
- Time required to complete the lesson.
- Teacher preparation and materials.
- Lecture/discussion—A complete teacher script for lectures including the title, introduction, body of the lecture and discussion questions are outlined.
- Learning activities—Descriptions of activities include the title, time required, introduction, procedure and closure.
- Student handouts.
- Homework assignments—The instructor is provided with the title, introduction, procedure and closure for presenting each homework assignment to the class.
- Diagrams—Diagrams of male and female anatomy and reproductive systems are presented.

Living Smart (Middle School) *(continued)*

Package Contents

- Teacher's manual.
- Complete set of overhead transparency masters for all lessons.
- Complete set of student handouts, parent materials and homework assignments.

Publisher Information

The University of Arkansas Press, Fayetteville, Arkansas 72701.

Sex Can Wait is available from ETR Associates, P.O. Box 1830, Santa Cruz, California 95061-1830; (800) 321-4407.

P.S.I. (Young Teens)

Title: *Postponing Sexual Involvement:*
An Educational Series for Young Teens
Authors: Marion Howard and Marie Mitchell
Year Developed: 1984
Latest Revision: 1990
Target Grade Level: Grades 7, 8 and 9
Length: 4 lessons, plus one reinforcement lesson to be conducted three months after the fourth lesson.
Cost: $80.00

Curriculum Description

Curriculum Focus

This curriculum was developed to provide young people with the tools to bridge the gap between physical development and their cognitive ability to handle the implications of such development. The primary emphasis is on skill building to carry out the general goal of saying "no," and on one's individual rights in relationships. The goals are for young people to:

- understand the pressures in our society which influence young people's sexual behavior
- understand their rights in social relationships
- deal with pressure situations through the use of assertive responses
- postpone sexual involvement

Lesson Format

Each lesson is presented as follows:

- Time.
- Supplies.
- Number in group—The authors suggest the number of students per activity.
- Seating—The arrangement of desks in the classroom is suggested for each lesson.
- Purpose of the lesson.
- Concepts.

57

- Lesson segments—For each concept in a lesson, the authors give the purpose of the lesson, approximate time needed, specific instructions to teach the activity, scripted lecture from the videocassette, questions for discussion, summary or closing and sample responses from the activity.
- Handouts—The authors provide a "Pressure Lines" handout in Lesson III and "Situations" handouts in Lesson IV.

Package Contents

- Educator's guide—Includes all lessons and student worksheets.
- Videocassette to be used in conjunction with the educator's guide.

Publisher Information

Emory/Grady Teen Services Program, Grady Memorial Hospital, 80 Butler Street, Atlanta, Georgia 30335-1801; (404) 616-3513.

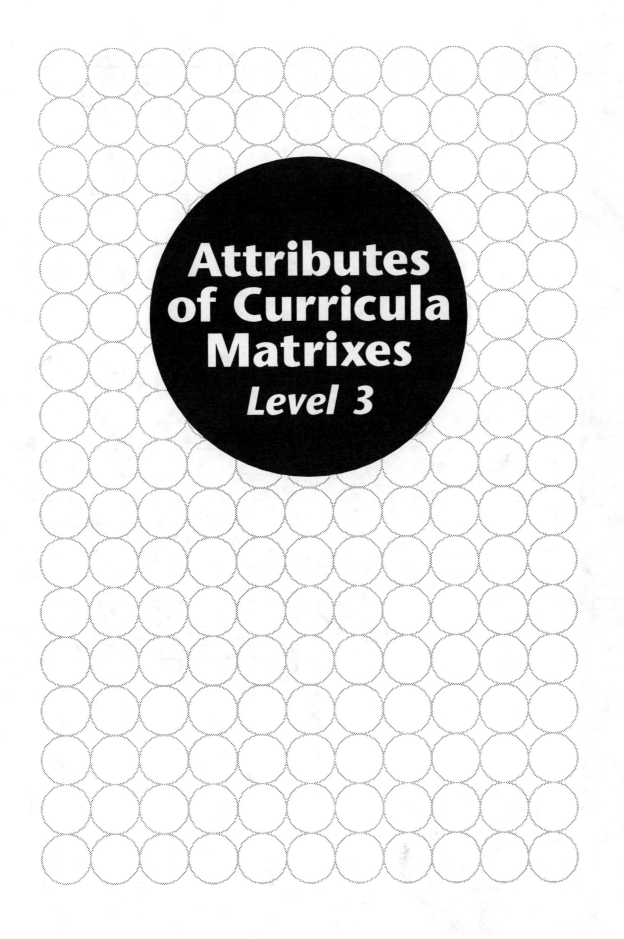

Attributes of Curricula Matrixes
Level 3

Attributes of Curricula

Level 3

Curriculum	Page Number	Puberty	Body Image	Gender Roles	Reproductive Anatomy/Physiology	Conception and Birth	Sexual Identity and Orientation	Relationships	Parenting	Sexual Expression	STD Transmission	HIV Transmission	Abstinence	Pregnancy Prevention	STD Prevention	HIV Prevention	Sexual Exploitation	Reproductive Health	Healthy Sexuality	Responsibility for Decisions	Abstinence (Philosophy)	Using Protection if Sexually Active	Philosophy Not Clear
3-R	41	✓		✓	✓		✓	✓			✓	✓	✓	✓	✓	✓	✓		✓	✓	✓		
Family Life	43		✓	✓	✓	✓	✓			✓	✓	✓	✓	✓	✓	✓	✓	✓	✓				
F.L.A.S.H. 7/8	45	✓		✓	✓	✓	✓	✓		✓	✓	✓	✓	✓	✓	✓	✓	✓	✓	✓	✓		
Healthy Sexuality	47	✓	✓	✓	✓	✓		✓		✓	✓	✓	✓	✓	✓			✓		✓	✓		
Values and Choices	49	✓	✓	✓	✓	✓	✓	✓		✓	✓	✓	✓	✓	✓	✓		✓	✓	✓	✓		
Into Adolescence	51	✓		✓	✓					✓	✓		✓		✓					✓			
Life Planning	53	✓	✓	✓	✓	✓	✓			✓	✓	✓			✓	✓			✓		✓		
Living Smart (Middle School)	55	✓	✓	✓	✓		✓	✓		✓	✓	✓								✓			
P.S.I. (Young Teens)	57	✓	✓	✓	✓	✓	✓	✓		✓	✓	✓								✓			

(For descriptions of attributes, see p. 63.)

Level 3 (continued)

Curriculum

Curriculum	Teaching Strategies													Skill-Building Strategies													
	Parent/Guardian Involvement	Peer Helper Component	Community Speakers/Involvement	Audiovisual Materials	Skills Practice and Rehearsal	Case Studies/Scenarios	Cooperative Learning/Small Groups	Journals/Story Writing	Student Worksheets	Large-Group Discussion	Teacher Lecture	Anonymous Question Box	Groundrules	Planning/Goal-Setting Skills	Decision-Making Skills	Conflict-Management Skills	Refusal Skills	Assertiveness Skills	General Communication Skills	Community Resources	Perceived STD/HIV Risk	Perceived Pregnancy Risk	Peer Norms	Consequences of Decisions	Influences on Decisions	Self-Awareness/Self-Esteem	Personal Values
3-R		✓			✓	✓			✓	✓	✓	✓	✓		✓	✓			✓	✓	✓	✓		✓	✓	✓	✓
Family Life		✓			✓	✓	✓			✓	✓	✓	✓			✓			✓	✓	✓	✓	✓			✓	✓
F.L.A.S.H. 7/8		✓		✓	✓	✓	✓		✓	✓	✓	✓	✓			✓		✓	✓	✓	✓	✓		✓	✓	✓	✓
Healthy Sexuality			✓	✓	✓	✓	✓	✓	✓	✓	✓					✓		✓	✓	✓	✓	✓	✓	✓	✓	✓	✓
Values and Choices		✓			✓	✓	✓		✓	✓	✓	✓	✓	✓	✓	✓		✓	✓	✓	✓	✓	✓		✓	✓	✓
Into Adolescence		✓		✓	✓	✓	✓		✓	✓	✓	✓	✓	✓	✓	✓			✓	✓	✓	✓		✓	✓	✓	✓
Life Planning				✓	✓	✓	✓		✓	✓	✓		✓	✓	✓	✓		✓	✓	✓	✓	✓			✓	✓	✓
Living Smart (Middle School)		✓			✓	✓	✓	✓	✓	✓	✓			✓	✓	✓		✓	✓			✓			✓	✓	✓
P.S.I. (Young Teens)			✓		✓	✓	✓	✓		✓	✓	✓	✓	✓		✓		✓									✓

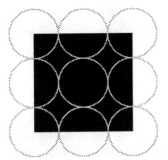

Descriptions
of Attributes

Content

Puberty

Physical changes that occur in males and females during puberty; individual differences in growth rates; feelings/emotions associated with changes during puberty.

Body Image

Individual variations in size, shape, etc.; uniqueness of each person; physical appearance as determined by heredity, environment, and health habits; disabilities; portrayal of body image by media; effect of physical appearance on how people interact with others.

Gender Roles

Messages from families, friends, media and society about how males and females should behave; both genders having similar talents, characteristics, strengths, hopes and need for equal opportunities; gender role stereotypes; laws protecting the rights of men and women.

Reproductive Anatomy/Physiology

Human body has capability to reproduce; body parts have correct names and specific functions; maturation of reproductive organs occurs at puberty; hormones influence sexual and reproductive function.

Conception and Birth

Union of sperm and egg in fertilization; heredity; pregnancy and development of the fetus; genetic disorders and birth defects; stages of birth; medical procedures and new reproductive technology.

Sexual Identity and Orientation

Attraction; definition of sexual orientation, including heterosexual, homosexual and bisexual; theories about what determines sexual orientation; mistreatment and denial of rights based on sexual orientation; support services for questioning youth.

Relationships

Definition of family; types of families; roles and responsibilities of family members; friendships with people of both genders; expressing love and affection; dating; importance of honest and open communication; shared responsibility in marriage; divorce; community resources.

Parenting

Skills and information needed to make good parents; balance of parenting and full-time job; difficulties of being a teen parent; different types of parenting as children get older; raising a child with special needs.

Sexual Expression

Ways to show love and affection without having sex; natural physical response to touch; sexual response experienced differently by each person; masturbation, fantasy and shared sexual behavior; capacity to respond sexually throughout life.

STD Transmission

Causes of sexually transmitted disease; modes of transmission; signs and symptoms; long-term effects of untreated STD; importance of open communication with partner; community resources for testing, treatment and counseling; hotlines.

HIV Transmission

Type of sexually transmitted disease; caused by human immunodeficiency virus (HIV); modes of transmission; signs and symptoms; differences from other STD; community resources for testing, treatment and counseling; hotlines.

Abstinence

Safest, most effective method of preventing STD, HIV infection and pregnancy; advantages of choosing not to have sex; physical and emotional readiness for sexual intercourse; importance of open and honest communication; always having a choice; giving and receiving pleasure without having sex.

Pregnancy Prevention

Decisions to have children based on religious beliefs, personal values and cultural traditions; methods of contraception, including advantages, disadvantages and effective use; individual responsibility for getting and using protection; importance of honest and open communication with partner.

STD Prevention

Methods of STD prevention, including advantages, disadvantages and effective use; individual responsibility for getting and using protection; importance of honest and open communication with partner; community resources.

HIV Prevention

Methods of HIV infection prevention, including advantages, disadvantages and effective use; individual responsibility for getting and using protection; importance of honest and open communication with partner; community resources.

Sexual Exploitation

Sexual harassment; sexual abuse; acquaintance rape; other types of sexual exploitation; individual rights related to any type of sexual exploitation; protecting oneself, including avoiding potentially dangerous situations and learning self-defense; community resources; support services.

Reproductive Health

Individual responsibility for health; importance of cleanliness, nutrition and exercise; routine physical examination; breast self-examination; testicular self-examination; prenatal effects of smoking, drinking and using other substances; birth defects and genetic counseling.

Philosophy

Promotes Healthy Sexuality

The curriculum presents sexuality as a natural and healthy part of everyday living. It is maintained that each person expresses his or her sexuality in a variety of ways based on personal background and experience. The curriculum addresses the physical, psychological, emotional, social, ethical and spiritual dimensions of healthy sexuality.

Promotes Responsibility for Decisions

The curriculum supports each individual's right and obligation to make decisions about his or her sexuality. The curriculum empowers young people to make responsible decisions by helping them examine internal and external influences on personal decisions, recognize short- and long-term consequences of their decisions for themselves and others, and access information and services through personal support systems and community resources.

Promotes Abstinence

The curriculum presents abstinence as the safest, most effective way to prevent sexually transmitted disease, HIV infection and pregnancy. It addresses the advantages of choosing not to have sexual intercourse, the benefits of delaying sex, and the risks of having sex if a person is not ready or does not want to.

Promotes Using Protection If Sexually Active

The curriculum acknowledges that some young people will have sexual intercourse and presents methods of protection from sexually transmitted disease, HIV infection and pregnancy. It discusses advantages, disadvantages and effectiveness of these methods.

Philosophy Not Clear

The curriculum has no clear focus.

Skill-Building Strategies

Examining Personal Values

The curriculum includes activities that help young people identify what they believe, what they think is important, and how personal values affect their sexuality-related decisions.

Increasing Self-Awareness/Building Self-Esteem

The curriculum includes activities that help young people become aware of their likes and dislikes, capabilities and limitations, talents and skills; appreciate their own uniqueness; and accept individual differences.

Examining Influences on Decisions

The curriculum includes activities that focus on the internal influences (wanting to be accepted, be part of a group, take risks, feel normal, feel good, etc.) and external influences (parents/caregivers, other adults, peers, media) that affect sexuality-related decisions.

Identifying Consequences of Decisions

The curriculum includes activities that help young people look at short- and long-term physical, emotional, social and legal consequences of sexuality-related decisions for themselves and others.

Addressing Peer Norms

The curriculum includes activities that allow young people to share their perceptions of norms related to abstinence and use of protection, and that promote changes in the normative message (e.g., making posters and pamphlets to support the message that "not everyone is doing it").

Examining Perceived Pregnancy Risk

The curriculum includes activities to help young people examine the risk of getting pregnant (based on specific behaviors) and understand how they can change their behaviors to decrease the probability of pregnancy.

Examining Perceived STD/HIV Risk

The curriculum includes activities to help young people examine the risk of getting a sexually transmitted disease, including HIV, and understand how they can change their behaviors to reduce the risk of becoming infected with STD/HIV.

Sexuality Education Curricula: The Consumer's Guide

Accessing Community Resources

The curriculum includes activities that help young people identify sources of information and services in the community, including community agencies, hotlines, clinics and support groups.

Building General Communication Skills

The curriculum includes activities where young people learn to communicate clearly—verbally and nonverbally; to listen actively; and to express their thoughts, feelings, attitudes, beliefs, values and ideas about sexuality-related issues.

Building Assertiveness Skills

The curriculum includes activities that give young people practice in saying what they think and standing up for what they believe, without hurting or denying the rights of others. It also helps students understand the differences between passive, assertive and aggressive responses.

Building Refusal Skills

The curriculum includes activities that help young people practice effective ways to say "no" without jeopardizing their peer and family relationships.

Building Conflict-Management Skills

The curriculum includes activities that help young people solve problems and resolve conflicts in relationships without using guilt, anger and/or intimidation. It also provides opportunities to practice negotiation skills.

Building Decision-Making Skills

The curriculum includes activities that help young people examine real-life situations, generate possible solutions, and anticipate the short- and long-term consequences of having sex and having unprotected sex, as well as understand how each decision can affect subsequent decisions.

Building Planning/Goal-Setting Skills

The curriculum includes activities that help young people examine personal expectations and those of others, identify short- and long-term personal goals, and identify barriers to achieving their personal goals. It also provides opportunities to use planning skills in situations related to having sex or having unprotected sex.

Teaching Strategies

Groundrules

With student input, the teacher establishes groundrules for classroom discussion of sexuality-related issues.

Anonymous Question Box

An anonymous question box is set up so that students can ask questions or express feelings and concerns without fear of embarrassment.

Teacher Lecture

The teacher provides key information directly to students with a minimum of class participation and interruption.

Large-Group Discussion

In an open discussion involving the entire class, students are guided by the teacher to share ideas, thoughts and beliefs about a sexuality-related issue.

Student Worksheets

A variety of written questions or forms are used to help students focus on particular topics. This strategy allows the sharing of opinions and ideas without having to discuss them openly with the rest of the class.

Journals/Story Writing

Students are given opportunities to write their thoughts and feelings about the sexuality-related issues discussed in class in personal journals or diaries.

Cooperative Learning/Small Groups

Lessons include small-group discussions about sexuality-related issues. Students are assigned certain roles and responsibilities within the group.

Case Studies/Scenarios

Lessons include case studies and real-life scenarios to help students practice personal and social skills.

Skills Practice and Rehearsal

Students are given a variety of opportunities to practice newly learned personal and social skills, including roleplays, small-group activities and worksheets.

Audiovisual Materials

The teacher uses audiovisual materials when presenting information and/or skills (transparencies, videos, slides, films, etc.).

Community Speakers/Involvement

Outside speakers from community agencies are asked to present sexuality-related information or skills.

Peer Helper Component

Same-age or cross-age peers are used in the presentation of sexuality-related information or skills.

Parent/Guardian Involvement

Homework assignments and curriculum activities are designed to be completed by parents or caregivers and their children.

Evaluation
of Curricula
Matrix
Level 3

Evaluation of Curricula

Level 3

Evaluation Criteria

- Comprehensiveness (Breadth)
- Comprehensiveness (Depth)
- Content Accuracy/Currency
- Skill-Building Variety (Breadth)
- Skill-Building Variety (Depth)
- Methods Variety
- Developmental Appropriateness
- Cultural Sensitivity
- Ease of Implementation
- Evaluation
- Appearance/Production Quality
- Overall Quality

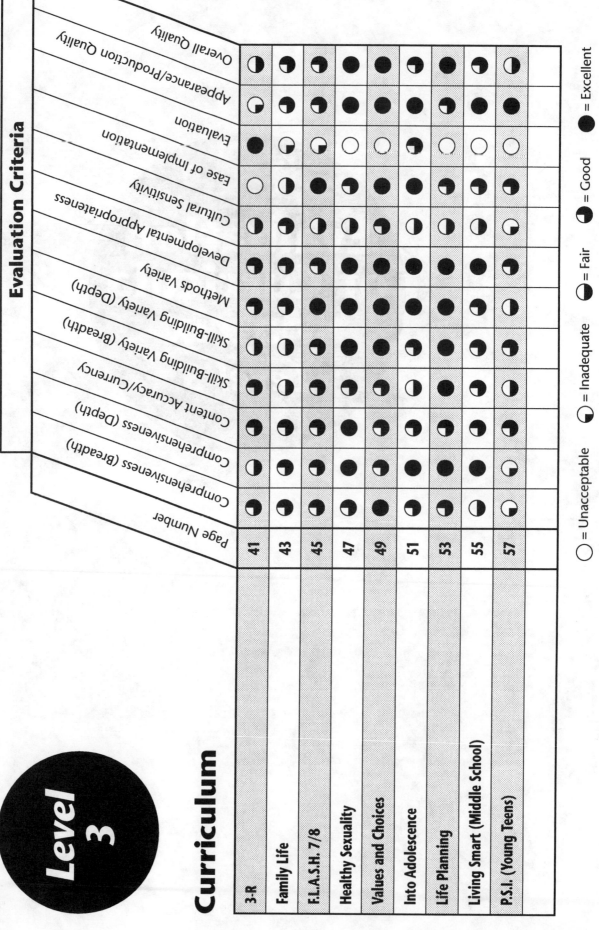

Curriculum

Curriculum	Page Number
3-R	41
Family Life	43
F.L.A.S.H. 7/8	45
Healthy Sexuality	47
Values and Choices	49
Into Adolescence	51
Life Planning	53
Living Smart (Middle School)	55
P.S.I. (Young Teens)	57

○ = Unacceptable ◔ = Inadequate ◑ = Fair ◕ = Good ● = Excellent

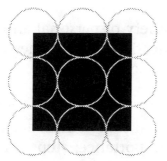

Descriptions of Evaluation Criteria

Evaluation Criteria

Comprehensiveness (Breadth)

The curriculum includes *all* developmentally appropriate key concepts as described by the *Guidelines for Comprehensive Sexuality Education* (National Guidelines Task Force, 1991).

Comprehensiveness (Depth)

The curriculum includes *all* subconcepts and developmental messages within each key concept as described by the *Guidelines for Comprehensive Sexuality Education* (National Guidelines Task Force, 1991).

Content Accuracy/Currency

The curriculum provides accurate information about sexuality-related topics and is based on current research and theory. Graphs, charts and tables are current and representative of the target population.

The curriculum is up to date and presents information in ways that interest today's young people. Graphs, charts, language and pictures reflect current issues and trends.

Skill-Building Variety (Breadth)

The curriculum provides activities to build a variety of personal and social skills: decision-making, general communication, assertiveness, refusal, conflict management and planning/goal-setting skills.

Skill-Building Variety (Depth)

The curriculum addresses each personal and social skill comprehensively: the skill is introduced focusing on its importance; steps for skill development are presented; the skill is modeled for students; the skill is practiced and rehearsed with a variety of situations; and feedback/reinforcement is provided.

Methods Variety

To meet the diverse needs and learning styles of students, the curriculum provides a variety of instructional strategies for providing key information; encouraging creative expression; sharing thoughts, feelings and opinions; and developing critical thinking skills.

Developmental Appropriateness

The curriculum presents sexuality-related information, instructional strategies, and personal and social skills appropriate for the cognitive, emotional and social developmental level and personal experience of the targeted grades. Lessons are adaptable to individual student needs.

Cultural Sensitivity

The curriculum does not contain information or activities that are biased in terms of race or ethnicity, sex or gender roles, family types, sexual orientation, and/or age. It portrays a variety of social groups and lifestyles in its examples, pictures and descriptions. Instructional strategies take into account the cultural and ethnic values, customs and practices of the community.

Ease of Implementation

The curriculum includes features that make it "user friendly." That is, all materials and master copies necessary for implementation are included; it is well organized, with clear, thorough instructions; it can easily be updated; and it provides references and support materials for teachers.

Evaluation

The curriculum provides methods for evaluating levels of student knowledge, attitudes and/or skills that are consistent with curriculum goals and lesson objectives.

Appearance/Production Quality

The curriculum is clearly written, up to date, aesthetically pleasing (including print quality), and likely to elicit student interest.

Overall Quality

Overall assessment of the quality of the curriculum is based on scores in comprehensiveness, content accuracy/currency, skill-building variety, methods variety, developmental appropriateness, cultural sensitivity, ease of implementation, evaluation and appearance/ production quality.

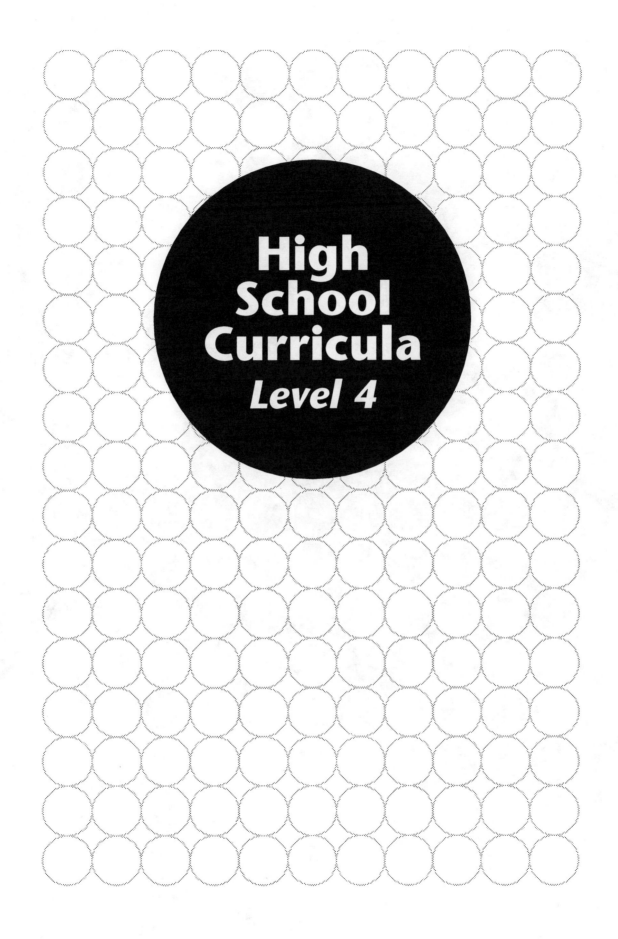

High
School
Curricula
Level 4

Entering Adulthood

Titles: 1. *Understanding Reproduction, Birth and Contraception*
2. *Coping with Sexual Pressures*
3. *Preventing Sexually Related Disease*

Authors:
1. Clint E. Bruess and Susan J. Laing
2. Nancy Abbey and Elizabeth Raptis Picco
3. Betty Hubbard

Year Developed: 1989

Latest Revision: None

Target Grade Level: Grades 9 through 12

Length:
1. 9 lessons
2. 7 lessons (Note: Authors suggest 3 core lessons—Lessons 2, 4 and 6—in the event that not all seven can be taught)
3. 6 lessons

Cost: $23.50 per module

Curriculum Description

Curriculum Focus

Information about sexuality is not harmful; students need to become comfortable in discussing these issues with other individuals and in groups. Students need to be aware that sexual abstinence ("voluntary avoidance of sexual intercourse") is a viable choice for teens and that sexual intercourse for most teens is not in their best interest. Finally, the risk of contracting an STD should be considered by teens in making choices about sexual behavior.

The modules listed here are those in the *Entering Adulthood* component of the Contemporary Health Series that deal with sexuality. *Understanding Reproduction* provides a foundation for decisions related to reproductive functioning and conception control. *Coping with Sexual Pressure* focuses on three core principles: (1) that sexual desires must be acknowledged to understand decisions concerning whether or not to have sex, (2) that young people need to express their love in ways other than intercourse and (3) that the capacity to delay intercourse is related to the ability to have power over one's life. *Preventing Sexually Related Disease* is primarily concerned with STD, abstinence, methods of protection and sources of treatment.

Other modules in the series present related and additional content and skills.

Lesson Format

The format for each lesson is as follows:

- Objectives.
- Time.
- Overview.
- Teacher materials and preparation.
- Key points.
- Procedure.
- Evaluation—A student assignment based on the key concept.
- Follow-up/extension activities—A follow-up lecture or activity is provided to aid in transition to the next lesson and to review key concepts.
- Teacher preparation and Background Information—Materials needed and teacher information regarding male and female anatomy, birth, contraception and STD.
- Diagrams/Handouts—Diagrams are provided for anatomy, male circumcision and use of birth control methods. "Comic" hand-outs/transparencies and symptoms charts are given.
- Student worksheets—worksheets for students are given in most lessons.

Package Contents

Each module provides background information about a specific aspect of sexuality; groundrules and realistic expectations; a list of the lessons and their related objectives; a glossary of terms and definitions; and a student workbook. *Coping with Sexual Pressure* contains a rationale for abstinence education, and parent/student worksheets.

Publisher Information

ETR Associates, PO Box 1830, Santa Cruz, California 95601; (800) 321-4407.

F.L.A.S.H. 9/10

Title: *F.L.A.S.H. (Family Life and Sexual Health) 9/10*
Author: Elizabeth Reiss
Year Developed: 1988
Latest Revision: 1989
Target Grade Level: Grades 9 and 10
Length: 30 lessons
Cost: $55.00

Curriculum Description

Curriculum Focus

The curriculum is based on "universal values" which are outlined specifically:

- Respect must be given for the individuality of the student and his or her peers in the classroom.
- Honest communication is fundamental in all relationships.
- People have a responsibility to learn as much as possible about themselves and others.

The goal is to enable individuals to become knowledgeable about human development and reproduction and to respect themselves and others.

Lesson Format

This is the foundation or core unit in a four-part curriculum designed for Grades 4 through 12. A supplemental unit for special education is an additional fifth unit component of the curriculum. Each lesson contains:

- Student learning objectives.
- Materials needed.
- Time needed to complete each lesson.
- Agenda with step-by-step procedures for teachers to follow.
- Activities section.

Package Contents

Included in each are a table of contents, unit philosophy and an overview of each lesson with objectives.

A resource guide for teachers provides additional sources of content knowledge. Tips for preparing parents and administrators, a sample syllabus and detailed field trip plans—including (1) sign-up sheets, (2) suggested types of trips, with related questions to ask, (3) suggested follow-up reports and (4) grading forms. Other items in the package are student reference sheets, family and individual homework exercises, unit tests with answer sheets, reproductive system transparency masters, games/simulations cards, case studies, student resource lists and roleplaying dialogues.

Publisher Information

Seattle–King County Department of Public Health, Family Planning Publications, 2124 4th Avenue, Seattle, Washington 98121; (206) 296-4672.

F.L.A.S.H. 11/12

Title: *F.L.A.S.H. (Family Life and Sexual Health) 11/12*
Author: Elizabeth Reiss
Year Developed: 1992
Lastest Revision: None
Target Grade Level: Grades 11 and 12
Length: 18 lessons
Cost: $40.00

Curriculum Description

Curriculum Focus

The curriculum is based on "universal values" which are outlined specifically:

- Respect must be given for the individuality of the student and his or her peers in the classroom.
- Honest communication is fundamental in all relationships.
- People have a responsibility to learn as much as possible about themselves and others.

The goal is to enable individuals to become knowledgeable about human development and reproduction and to respect themselves and others.

Lesson Format

Information in this curriculum builds upon material presented in F.L.A.S.H. 9/10. Included are four topical pretests to assess background knowledge. Suggestions and tips on how to teach the course are given in the introductions to each unit. Each lesson contains:

- Student learning objectives.
- Materials needed.
- Time needed to complete each lesson.
- Agenda with step-by-step procedures for teachers to follow.
- Activities section.

Package Contents

Specific graphics and masters for overhead transparencies are provided. Background factual information ("Student Reference Sheets") are provided for the reproductive systems. Each unit has a detailed appendix, including glossary terms used in the unit and footnotes. Lessons 2, 5, 10 and 14 have recommended videotapes that should accompany the lesson. Included in the teacher preparation introductory section are a sample agenda, field trip instructions and field trip sign-up sheets. The appendixes include sample parent letters, State of Washington regulations, community resources, a teacher's glossary and a F.L.A.S.H. curriculum overview for grades K through 12.

Publisher Information

Seattle–King County Department of Public Health, Family Planning Publications, 2124 4th Avenue, Seattle, Washington 98121; (206) 296-4672.

Just Say Know

Title: *Just Say Know: An Educator's Guide to Helping Young People Make Informed Decisions*

Author: Jennifer S. Shaw

Year Developed 1988

Latest Revision: None

Target Grade Level: Grades 9 through 12

Length: Lessons are not numbered. This curriculum is organized by four major subject areas. Each area contains approximately eight 30-minute to 1-hour activities. The total length could be approximated at 22 to 30 lessons.

Cost: $18.00

Curriculum Description

Curriculum Focus

This guide is based on a conceptual model of responsible decision making. Responsible sexual decisions require accurate information, clear values, communication, respect for others and an understanding of expectations and consequences of sexual intimacy, and the wisdom of postponing pregnancy until one can support a child. It is hoped that these factors will preserve students' physical and emotional wellness now and in the future.

Lesson Format

The following information is included within each lesson.

- Rationale.
- Objective.
- Activity—A thorough description of the learning activities from the review to the body of the lesson.
- Variation—Expands on the activities and suggests additional topics for class discussion.
- Discussion—Certain lessons include specific questions to probe with the class on particular topics.
- Evaluation—One to three specific evaluation questions for each lesson.

- Skills/time box—A box in the lower right-hand corner identifies the skills of the lesson in one word or phrase, along with the approximate time needed to complete the lesson.
- Worksheets—Presented following the lesson plan, coincide with the topic.

Package Contents

The introduction section to the teachers' guide includes a rationale for comprehensive sexuality education, list of universal values, objectives, parental involvement, teaching techniques, evaluation, values clarification, outside the school setting implementation and an index of activities categorized by the four major areas. The body of the curriculum is outlined in the format description above. The appendix provides information on sexuality education in Utah, adolescent sexuality in general, glossary and fact sheets on reproductive health, and media available through Planned Parenthood of Utah and community organizations in Utah.

Publishers Information

Planned Parenthood of Utah, 654 South 900 East, Salt Lake City, Utah 84102; (801) 532-1586.

Living Smart (H.S.)

Title: *Living Smart: Understanding Sexuality into Adulthood*
Authors: Pennie Core-Gebhart, Susan J. Hart
and Michael Young
Year Developed: 1991
Latest Revision: 1994 (Retitled *Sex Can Wait: An Abstinence-Based Sexuality Curriculum for High School*)
Target Grade Level: Grades 9 and 10
Length: 24 lessons
Cost: $59.95

Curriculum Description

Curriculum Focus

The primary goal is to promote abstinence and the concept that adolescent sexuality is a shared responsibility. Males and females need to develop both self and social understanding and factual knowledge about sexuality. Another goal is to involve the school, parents and community in assisting adolescents with development of critical life skills.

Lesson Format

Each lesson is presented as follows:
- Teaching objectives.
- Instructor background—Information on the topic for each lesson is provided for the instructor.
- Time required to complete the lesson.
- Teacher preparation and materials.
- Lecture/discussion—A complete teacher script for lectures including the title, introduction, body of the lecture and discussion questions are outlined.
- Learning activities—Descriptions of activities include the title, time required, introduction, procedure and closure.
- Student handouts.
- Homework assignments—The instructor is provided with the title, introduction, procedure and closure for presenting each homework assignment to the class.
- Diagrams—Diagrams of male and female anatomy and reproductive systems are presented.

Living Smart (H.S.) *(continued)*

Package Contents

- Teacher's manual.
- Complete set of overhead transparency masters for all lessons.
- Complete set of student handouts, parent materials and homework assignments.

Publisher Information

The University of Arkansas Press, Fayetteville, Arkansas 72701.

Sex Can Wait is available from ETR Associates, P.O. Box 1830, Santa Cruz, California 95061-1830; (800) 321-4407.

Positive Images

Title: *Positive Images: A New Approach to Contraceptive Education*

Authors: Peggy Brick and Carolyn Cooperman

Year Developed: 1986

Latest Revision: 1987

Target Grade Level: Grades 9 through 12

Length: 14 lessons

Cost: $19.95

Curriculum Description

Curriculum Focus

This program is not intended for use as a comprehensive sexuality curriculum. Its primary focus is to incorporate research findings surrounding effective contraceptive use by adolescents, including addressing both knowledge and social-psychological barriers. Activities are designed to make students active learners in the decision-making process related to becoming sexually involved (including saying "no") and using contraceptives.

Lesson Format

Each lesson briefly describes its purpose and rationale and lists the materials needed. Specific step-by-step procedures are given in each unit. Discussion questions are provided.

Package Contents

Teacher's manual with a resource section of videotape, visual aids, and book and pamphlet references. Sample worksheets are provided in the manual.

Publisher Information

The Center for Family Life Education, Planned Parenthood of Greater Northern New Jersey, 575 Main Street, Hackensack, New Jersey 07601; (201) 489-1265.

Reducing the Risk

Title: *Reducing the Risk: Building Skills to Prevent Pregnancy*
Author: Richard P. Barth
Year Developed: 1989
Latest Revision: 1993 (Retitled *Reducing the Risk: Building Skills to Prevent Pregnancy, HIV and STD*)
Target Grade Level: Grades 9 through 12
Length: 12 lessons
Cost: $42.95

Curriculum Description

Curriculum Focus

The curriculum is based upon research findings about reducing risks associated with sexual behavior, cited and explained in the introduction. It combines cognitive and social skill training. It is based on three major premises:

1. Abstaining from sexual activity or refusing unprotected sexual intercourse are the only responsible alternatives for teens.
2. Correct factual information about conception, contraception, HIV/AIDS and STD is essential for responsible sexual behavior.
3. Effective communication skills about abstinence and protection from risky sexual behavior are essential.

Lesson Format

The format for each lesson includes:

- Preparation—Teacher preparation responsibilities for the lesson are listed.
- Outline of activities—Each segment of the lesson, approximate time required for each activity and materials needed are sketched in a lesson plan format.
- Notes to the teacher—Notes are interspersed among certain lessons to provide teachers with cues for enhancing student discussions and hints for better activity management.
- Activities—Detailed steps for leading each activity are described, beginning with the Review activity, continuing with several activities for the new material and concluding with a lesson summary. Preceding homework is discussed as part of the review segment and new homework assignments are discussed prior to the lesson summary.

90

- Lesson summary—The lesson summary reminds students of the major concepts from the lesson and provides the transition to the next lesson.
- Handouts and worksheets—A variety of handouts and worksheets for in-class work, roleplays, quizzes and homework assignments are contained within each lesson.
- Lecture notes—Lesson 7 on contraception, and Lesson 12 on HIV/STD provide supplementary background information for teachers.

Prior to the actual 15-day curriculum, a one-day initiation lesson is provided. This lesson includes establishing groundrules and steps for securing parent notification and permission.

Package Contents

The teacher's manual includes all of the student worksheets, handouts, quizzes and supplementary lecture notes as described in the format. An order form on the last page of the manual lists supplementary teaching materials and pamphlets available for purchase. A student workbook with individual and group worksheets, homework assignments, roleplays and handouts is also available.

Publisher Information

ETR Associates, P. O. Box 1830, Santa Cruz, California 95061-1830; (800) 321-4407.

Teaching Safer Sex

Title: *Teaching Safer Sex*

Authors: Peggy Brick, Catherine Charlton, Hillary Kunins and Steve Brown

Year Developed: 1989

Latest Revision: None

Target Grade Level: Grade 12 to college level

Length: 21 lessons

Cost: $19.95

Curriculum Description

Curriculum Focus

This curriculum is not intended to be comprehensive in scope. It is designed to encourage behaviors that reduce the risk of unwanted consequences of sexual activity, including unwanted pregnancy and coercive sex. The primary purpose is to address knowledge, attitudes and skills required for such "safer" sexual behavior.

Lesson Format

Objectives, rationale and materials needed are listed for the lesson. A procedure section gives specific step-by-step instructions for teaching the lesson. Suggested discussion questions are included as well as follow-up activities to extend each lesson. A table of contents provides a brief description of each lesson, which identifies strategies addressed in each topic area.

Package Contents

An instructor's manual is provided along with a listing of available resources. The resource section includes print resources, books, curricula, pamphlets, booklets and lists of audiovisual publishers and distributors.

Publisher Information

The Center for Family Life Education, Planned Parenthood of Greater Northern New Jersey, Hackensack, New Jersey 07601; (201) 489-1265.

Making Healthy Choices

Title: *Understanding Sexuality: Making Healthy Choices*
(A comprehensive human sexuality curriculum for senior high school students)

Authors: Lucy Kapp, Gloria Ferguson, Sandy Naughton, Judy Bergh Palmer and Lynn Young

Year Developed: 1988

Latest Revision: None

Target Grade Level: Grades 9 through 12

Target Grade Level: 16 lessons

Cost: $39.95

Curriculum Description

Curriculum Focus

This comprehensive sexuality education curriculum can be used independently or as a senior high sequel to *Values and Choices*. Its focus is to provide adolescents with guidance, information, and support to make responsible decisions about sexual behavior that impact their physical, mental and social well-being.

Lesson Format

Each lesson is presented as follows:

- Rationale.
- Goal.
- Learner outcomes (cognitive, affective and behavioral).
- Background information for teachers—Descriptions of the physical, mental and social developmental stages of the students as they relate to the topic; the teacher's role in the lesson; and suggestions for creating a comfortable classroom environment for discourse.
- Teacher preparation checklist.
- Learning activities.
- Teacher reference—Lesson 1 provides teacher responses to typical student questions, and Lesson 6 (on sexual orientation) and Lesson 12 (on STD) provide teachers with "Discussion Keys" for classroom use.
- Student worksheets—A variety of handouts are provided for individual and small group work.

Making Healthy Choices (continued)

Package Contents

- Teacher's Manual which includes a current list of audiovisual resources for specific lessons.
- Set of master handouts for each lesson.

Publisher Information

Health Start, 590 Park Street, Suite 208, St. Paul, Minnesota 55103-1843; (612) 221-3441.

Understanding Sexuality

Title: *Understanding Sexuality—*
A Teaching Module for High Schools
Authors: Jacquelyn G. Sowers, Ruth N. MacDonald
and William D. Sowers
Year Developed: 1986
Latest Revision: 1990 (4th Edition)
Target Grade Level: Grades 9 through 12
Length: 14 lessons, 1 to 2 days per lesson
Cost: See note below

Curriculum Description

Curriculum Focus

This curriculum stresses that the topics of sexuality and the meaning of intimacy in relationships are essential to comprehensive school health education. The basic messages of the curriculum are to

- Treat adolescents with respect as emerging adults.
- Recognize adolescents' healthy need to understand sexuality.
- Provide accurate information necessary to make intelligent decisions.
- Acknowledge and support values of home and church.
- Provide information on community resources that can assist adolescents with sexual matters.
- Encourage postponing sexual intercourse.

Lesson Format

Each lesson contains the following items:
- Lesson objectives.
- Lesson preview—An introduction to the lesson is provided for the instructor to inform students prior to beginning the lesson.
- Lesson preparation.
- Lesson plan—Step-by-step narrative of the lesson from the introduction to closure.
- Teacher notes—Background information on the lesson content.
- Student worksheets, diagrams and handouts.

Package Contents

- Curriculum Guide includes curriculum overview and goals, and a module overview of each lesson and its description.
- Packet of supplementary masters for duplicating.
- Video: "Teenage Father" (30 minutes).

Publisher Information

Sopris West Inc., 1140 Boston Avenue, Longmont, Colorado 80501; (303) 651-2829.

Note: To adopt this curriculum a school district must send a team of six to ten professionals from their school district for training. The team should be comprised of an administrator, a school nurse, a parent and teachers. The cost of the three-day training and three manuals for the team is $1000.00. After the initial three-day team training, the cost for an individual teacher to train is $160.00.

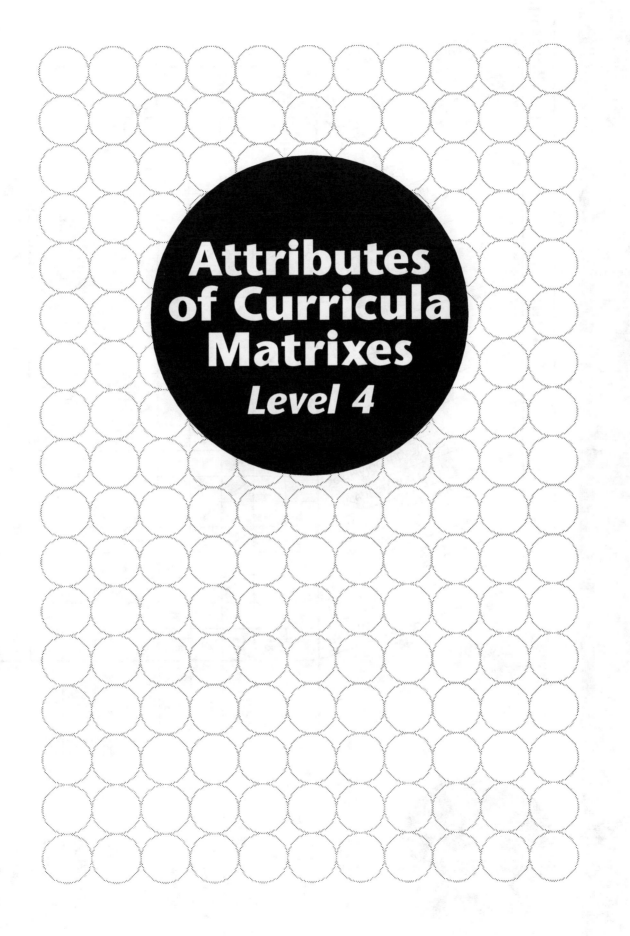

Attributes
of Curricula
Matrixes
Level 4

Attributes of Curricula

Level 4

Curriculum	Philosophy Not Clear	Using Protection if Sexually Active	Abstinence	Responsibility for Decisions	Healthy Sexuality	Reproductive Health	Sexual Exploitation	HIV Prevention	STD Prevention	Pregnancy Prevention	Abstinence	HIV Transmission	STD Transmission	Sexual Expression	Parenting	Relationships	Sexual Identity and Orientation	Conception and Birth	Reproductive Anatomy/Physiology	Gender Roles	Body Image	Puberty	Page Number
Entering Adulthood			✓	✓	✓		✓	✓	✓	✓	✓	✓	✓	✓		✓	✓			✓			79
F.L.A.S.H. 9/10			✓	✓	✓	✓	✓	✓	✓	✓	✓	✓	✓	✓		✓	✓			✓	✓		81
F.L.A.S.H. 11/12			✓	✓	✓	✓	✓	✓	✓	✓	✓	✓	✓	✓		✓	✓			✓	✓		83
Just Say Know				✓	✓	✓		✓	✓	✓	✓	✓	✓	✓		✓	✓			✓	✓	✓	85
Living Smart (H.S.)				✓				✓		✓	✓	✓				✓	✓				✓		87
Positive Images			✓		✓					✓	✓				✓				✓		✓		89
Reducing the Risk			✓	✓					✓	✓	✓	✓	✓	✓		✓					✓		90
Teaching Safer Sex			✓		✓			✓	✓	✓		✓	✓	✓			✓		✓	✓	✓		92
Making Healthy Choices			✓		✓			✓	✓	✓	✓	✓	✓	✓		✓	✓		✓	✓	✓		93
Understanding Sexuality			✓	✓		✓			✓	✓	✓	✓	✓	✓		✓	✓	✓	✓	✓	✓		95

* Not appropriate for this age group.

(For descriptions of attributes, see p. 101.)

Level 4 (continued)

Curriculum

Curriculum	Parent/Guardian Involvement	Peer Helper Component	Community Speakers/Involvement	Audiovisual Materials	Skills Practice and Rehearsal	Case Studies/Scenarios	Cooperative Learning/Small Groups	Journals/Story Writing	Student Worksheets	Large-Group Discussion	Teacher Lecture	Anonymous Question Box	Groundrules	Planning/Goal-Setting Skills	Decision-Making Skills	Conflict-Management Skills	Refusal Skills	Assertiveness Skills	General Communication Skills	Community Resources	Perceived STD/HIV Risk	Perceived Pregnancy Risk	Peer Norms	Consequences of Decisions	Influences on Decisions	Self-Awareness/Self-Esteem	Personal Values
Entering Adulthood	✓			✓	✓	✓	✓	✓	✓	✓	✓		✓	✓	✓	✓		✓			✓	✓		✓	✓	✓	
F.L.A.S.H. 9/10	✓			✓	✓	✓	✓	✓		✓	✓	✓	✓	✓	✓				✓	✓	✓	✓			✓	✓	✓
F.L.A.S.H. 11/12	✓		✓	✓	✓	✓	✓	✓		✓	✓	✓	✓	✓	✓	✓			✓	✓	✓			✓	✓	✓	✓
Just Say Know	✓				✓	✓	✓	✓		✓	✓	✓	✓	✓	✓					✓	✓		✓		✓		✓
Living Smart (H.S.)	✓				✓	✓	✓	✓		✓	✓	✓	✓	✓	✓	✓		✓	✓		✓	✓		✓	✓	✓	✓
Positive Images						✓	✓	✓		✓	✓									✓				✓		✓	
Reducing the Risk	✓				✓	✓	✓	✓		✓	✓	✓			✓	✓			✓	✓	✓	✓		✓	✓	✓	
Teaching Safer Sex					✓	✓	✓	✓		✓	✓				✓				✓	✓	✓		✓		✓	✓	
Making Healthy Choices			✓	✓	✓	✓	✓	✓		✓	✓	✓		✓									✓			✓	✓
Understanding Sexuality	✓		✓	✓	✓		✓	✓	✓	✓	✓	✓													✓	✓	✓

Teaching Strategies | **Skill-Building Strategies**

Descriptions of Attributes

Content

Puberty

Physical changes that occur in males and females during puberty; individual differences in growth rates; feelings/emotions associated with changes during puberty.

Body Image

Individual variations in size, shape, etc.; uniqueness of each person; physical appearance as determined by heredity, environment, and health habits; disabilities; portrayal of body image by media; effect of physical appearance on how people interact with others.

Gender Roles

Messages from families, friends, media and society about how males and females should behave; both genders having similar talents, characteristics, strengths, hopes and need for equal opportunities; gender role stereotypes; laws protecting the rights of men and women.

Reproductive Anatomy/Physiology

Human body has capability to reproduce; body parts have correct names and specific functions; maturation of reproductive organs occurs at puberty; hormones influence sexual and reproductive function.

Conception and Birth

Union of sperm and egg in fertilization; heredity; pregnancy and development of the fetus; genetic disorders and birth defects; stages of birth; medical procedures and new reproductive technology.

Sexual Identity and Orientation

Attraction; definition of sexual orientation, including heterosexual, homosexual and bisexual; theories about what determines sexual orientation; mistreatment and denial of rights based on sexual orientation; support services for questioning youth.

Relationships

Definition of family; types of families; roles and responsibilities of family members; friendships with people of both genders; expressing love and affection; dating; importance of honest and open communication; shared responsibility in marriage; divorce; community resources.

Parenting

Skills and information needed to make good parents; balance of parenting and full-time job; difficulties of being a teen parent; different types of parenting as children get older; raising a child with special needs.

Sexual Expression

Ways to show love and affection without having sex; natural physical response to touch; sexual response experienced differently by each person; masturbation, fantasy and shared sexual behavior; capacity to respond sexually throughout life.

STD Transmission

Causes of sexually transmitted disease; modes of transmission; signs and symptoms; long-term effects of untreated STD; importance of open communication with partner; community resources for testing, treatment and counseling; hotlines.

HIV Transmission

Type of sexually transmitted disease; caused by human immunodeficiency virus (HIV); modes of transmission; signs and symptoms; differences from other STD; community resources for testing, treatment and counseling; hotlines.

Abstinence

Safest, most effective method of preventing STD, HIV infection and pregnancy; advantages of choosing not to have sex; physical and emotional readiness for sexual intercourse; importance of open and honest communication; always having a choice; giving and receiving pleasure without having sex.

Pregnancy Prevention

Decisions to have children based on religious beliefs, personal values and cultural traditions; methods of contraception, including advantages, disadvantages and effective use; individual responsibility for getting and using protection; importance of honest and open communication with partner.

STD Prevention

Methods of STD prevention, including advantages, disadvantages and effective use; individual responsibility for getting and using protection; importance of honest and open communication with partner; community resources.

HIV Prevention

Methods of HIV infection prevention, including advantages, disadvantages and effective use; individual responsibility for getting and using protection; importance of honest and open communication with partner; community resources.

Sexual Exploitation

Sexual harassment; sexual abuse; acquaintance rape; other types of sexual exploitation; individual rights related to any type of sexual exploitation; protecting oneself, including avoiding potentially dangerous situations and learning self-defense; community resources; support services.

Reproductive Health

Individual responsibility for health; importance of cleanliness, nutrition and exercise; routine physical examination; breast self-examination; testicular self-examination; prenatal effects of smoking, drinking and using other substances; birth defects and genetic counseling.

Philosophy

Promotes Healthy Sexuality

The curriculum presents sexuality as a natural and healthy part of everyday living. It is maintained that each person expresses his or her sexuality in a variety of ways based on personal background and experience. The curriculum addresses the physical, psychological, emotional, social, ethical and spiritual dimensions of healthy sexuality.

Promotes Responsibility for Decisions

The curriculum supports each individual's right and obligation to make decisions about his or her sexuality. The curriculum empowers young people to make responsible decisions by helping them examine internal and external influences on personal decisions, recognize short- and long-term consequences of their decisions for themselves and others, and access information and services through personal support systems and community resources.

Promotes Abstinence

The curriculum presents abstinence as the safest, most effective way to prevent sexually transmitted disease, HIV infection and pregnancy. It addresses the advantages of choosing not to have sexual intercourse, the benefits of delaying sex, and the risks of having sex if a person is not ready or does not want to.

Promotes Using Protection If Sexually Active

The curriculum acknowledges that some young people will have sexual intercourse and presents methods of protection from sexually transmitted disease, HIV infection and pregnancy. It discusses advantages, disadvantages and effectiveness of these methods.

Philosophy Not Clear

The curriculum has no clear focus.

Descriptions of Attributes

Skill-Building Strategies

Examining Personal Values

The curriculum includes activities that help young people identify what they believe, what they think is important, and how personal values affect their sexuality-related decisions.

Increasing Self-Awareness/Building Self-Esteem

The curriculum includes activities that help young people become aware of their likes and dislikes, capabilities and limitations, talents and skills; appreciate their own uniqueness; and accept individual differences.

Examining Influences on Decisions

The curriculum includes activities that focus on the internal influences (wanting to be accepted, be part of a group, take risks, feel normal, feel good, etc.) and external influences (parents/caregivers, other adults, peers, media) that affect sexuality-related decisions.

Identifying Consequences of Decisions

The curriculum includes activities that help young people look at short- and long-term physical, emotional, social and legal consequences of sexuality-related decisions for themselves and others.

Addressing Peer Norms

The curriculum includes activities that allow young people to share their perceptions of norms related to abstinence and use of protection, and that promote changes in the normative message (e.g., making posters and pamphlets to support the message that "not everyone is doing it").

Examining Perceived Pregnancy Risk

The curriculum includes activities to help young people examine the risk of getting pregnant (based on specific behaviors) and understand how they can change their behaviors to decrease the probability of pregnancy.

Examining Perceived STD/HIV Risk

The curriculum includes activities to help young people examine the risk of getting a sexually transmitted disease, including HIV, and understand how they can change their behaviors to reduce the risk of becoming infected with STD/HIV.

Accessing Community Resources

The curriculum includes activities that help young people identify sources of information and services in the community, including community agencies, hotlines, clinics and support groups.

Building General Communication Skills

The curriculum includes activities where young people learn to communicate clearly—verbally and nonverbally; to listen actively; and to express their thoughts, feelings, attitudes, beliefs, values and ideas about sexuality-related issues.

Building Assertiveness Skills

The curriculum includes activities that give young people practice in saying what they think and standing up for what they believe, without hurting or denying the rights of others. It also helps students understand the differences between passive, assertive and aggressive responses.

Building Refusal Skills

The curriculum includes activities that help young people practice effective ways to say "no" without jeopardizing their peer and family relationships.

Building Conflict-Management Skills

The curriculum includes activities that help young people solve problems and resolve conflicts in relationships without using guilt, anger and/or intimidation. It also provides opportunities to practice negotiation skills.

Building Decision-Making Skills

The curriculum includes activities that help young people examine real-life situations, generate possible solutions, and anticipate the short- and long-term consequences of having sex and having unprotected sex, as well as understand how each decision can affect subsequent decisions.

Building Planning/Goal-Setting Skills

The curriculum includes activities that help young people examine personal expectations and those of others, identify short- and long-term personal goals, and identify barriers to achieving their personal goals. It also provides opportunities to use planning skills in situations related to having sex or having unprotected sex.

Teaching Strategies

Groundrules

With student input, the teacher establishes groundrules for classroom discussion of sexuality-related issues.

Anonymous Question Box

An anonymous question box is set up so that students can ask questions or express feelings and concerns without fear of embarrassment.

Teacher Lecture

The teacher provides key information directly to students with a minimum of class participation and interruption.

Large-Group Discussion

In an open discussion involving the entire class, students are guided by the teacher to share ideas, thoughts and beliefs about a sexuality-related issue.

Student Worksheets

A variety of written questions or forms are used to help students focus on particular topics. This strategy allows the sharing of opinions and ideas without having to discuss them openly with the rest of the class.

Journals/Story Writing

Students are given opportunities to write their thoughts and feelings about the sexuality-related issues discussed in class in personal journals or diaries.

Cooperative Learning/Small Groups

Lessons include small-group discussions about sexuality-related issues. Students are assigned certain roles and responsibilities within the group.

Case Studies/Scenarios

Lessons include case studies and real-life scenarios to help students practice personal and social skills.

Skills Practice and Rehearsal

Students are given a variety of opportunities to practice newly learned personal and social skills, including roleplays, small-group activities and worksheets.

Audiovisual Materials

The teacher uses audiovisual materials when presenting information and/or skills (transparencies, videos, slides, films, etc.).

Community Speakers/Involvement

Outside speakers from community agencies are asked to present sexuality-related information or skills.

Peer Helper Component

Same-age or cross-age peers are used in the presentation of sexuality-related information or skills.

Parent/Guardian Involvement

Homework assignments and curriculum activities are designed to be completed by parents or caregivers and their children.

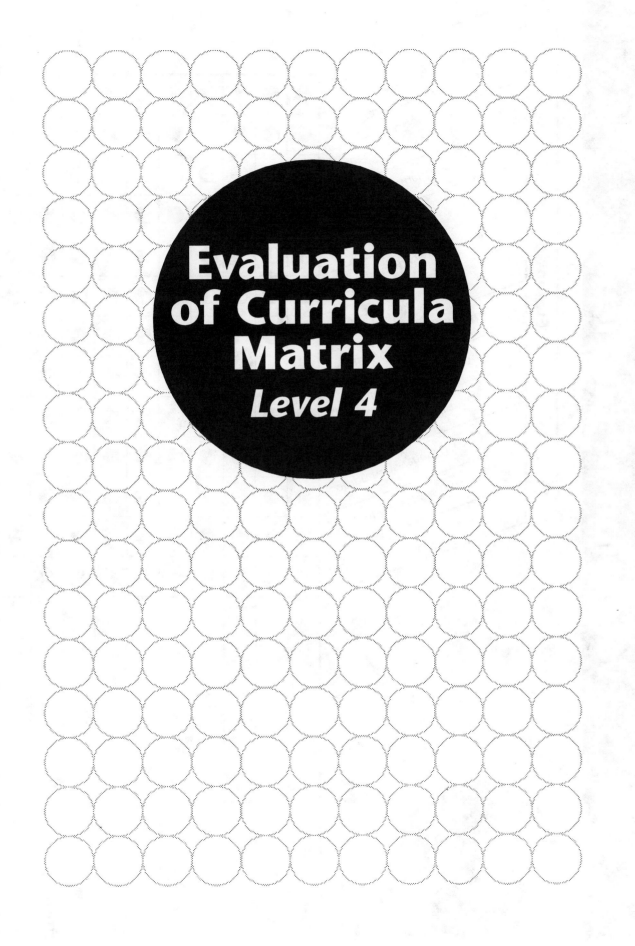

Evaluation
of Curricula
Matrix
Level 4

Evaluation of Curricula

Level 4

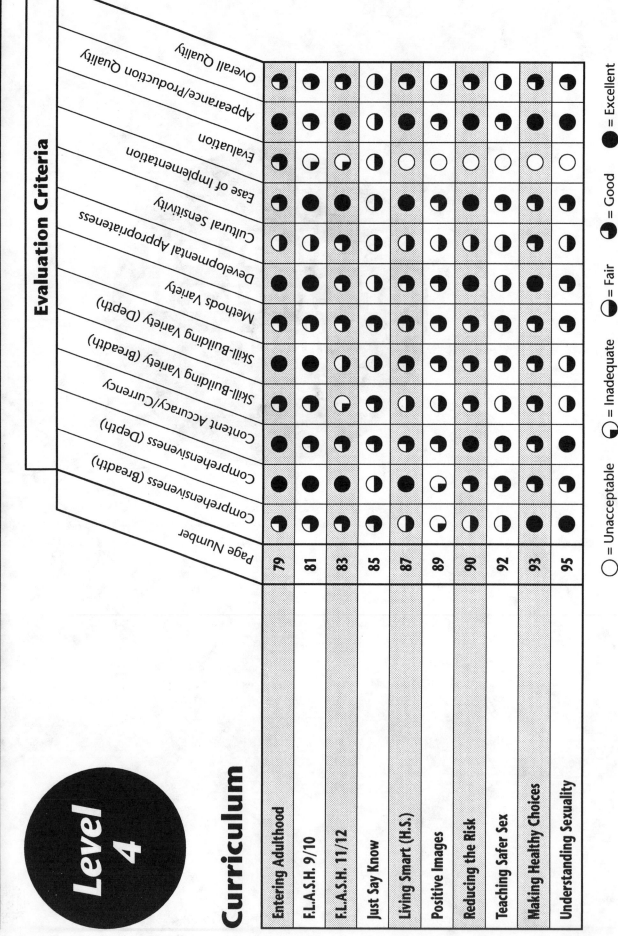

Evaluation Criteria

Curriculum / Page Number / Comprehensiveness (Breadth) / Comprehensiveness (Depth) / Content Accuracy/Currency / Skill-Building Variety (Breadth) / Skill-Building Variety (Depth) / Methods Variety / Developmental Appropriateness / Cultural Sensitivity / Ease of Implementation / Evaluation / Appearance/Production Quality / Overall Quality

Curriculum

Curriculum	Page Number
Entering Adulthood	79
F.L.A.S.H. 9/10	81
F.L.A.S.H. 11/12	83
Just Say Know	85
Living Smart (H.S.)	87
Positive Images	89
Reducing the Risk	90
Teaching Safer Sex	92
Making Healthy Choices	93
Understanding Sexuality	95

Legend:
○ = Unacceptable   ◔ = Inadequate   ◑ = Fair   ◕ = Good   ● = Excellent

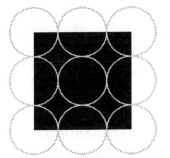

Descriptions of Evaluation Criteria

Evaluation Criteria

Comprehensiveness (Breadth)

The curriculum includes *all* developmentally appropriate key concepts as described by the *Guidelines for Comprehensive Sexuality Education* (National Guidelines Task Force, 1991).

Comprehensiveness (Depth)

The curriculum includes *all* subconcepts and developmental messages within each key concept as described by the *Guidelines for Comprehensive Sexuality Education* (National Guidelines Task Force, 1991).

Content Accuracy/Currency

The curriculum provides accurate information about sexuality-related topics and is based on current research and theory. Graphs, charts and tables are current and representative of the target population.

The curriculum is up to date and presents information in ways that interest today's young people. Graphs, charts, language and pictures reflect current issues and trends.

Skill-Building Variety (Breadth)

The curriculum provides activities to build a variety of personal and social skills: decision-making, general communication, assertiveness, refusal, conflict management and planning/goal-setting skills.

Skill-Building Variety (Depth)

The curriculum addresses each personal and social skill comprehensively: the skill is introduced focusing on its importance; steps for skill development are presented; the skill is modeled for students; the skill is practiced and rehearsed with a variety of situations; and feedback/reinforcement is provided.

Methods Variety

To meet the diverse needs and learning styles of students, the curriculum provides a variety of instructional strategies for providing key information; encouraging creative expression; sharing thoughts, feelings and opinions; and developing critical thinking skills.

Developmental Appropriateness

The curriculum presents sexuality-related information, instructional strategies, and personal and social skills appropriate for the cognitive, emotional and social developmental level and personal experience of the targeted grades. Lessons are adaptable to individual student needs.

Cultural Sensitivity

The curriculum does not contain information or activities that are biased in terms of race or ethnicity, sex or gender roles, family types, sexual orientation, and/or age. It portrays a variety of social groups and lifestyles in its examples, pictures and descriptions. Instructional strategies take into account the cultural and ethnic values, customs and practices of the community.

Ease of Implementation

The curriculum includes features that make it "user friendly." That is, all materials and master copies necessary for implementation are included; it is well organized, with clear, thorough instructions; it can easily be updated; and it provides references and support materials for teachers.

Evaluation

The curriculum provides methods for evaluating levels of student knowledge, attitudes and/or skills that are consistent with curriculum goals and lesson objectives.

Appearance/Production Quality

The curriculum is clearly written, up to date, aesthetically pleasing (including print quality), and likely to elicit student interest.

Overall Quality

Overall assessment of the quality of the curriculum is based on scores in comprehensiveness, content accuracy/currency, skill-building variety, methods variety, developmental appropriateness, cultural sensitivity, ease of implementation, evaluation and appearance/production quality.

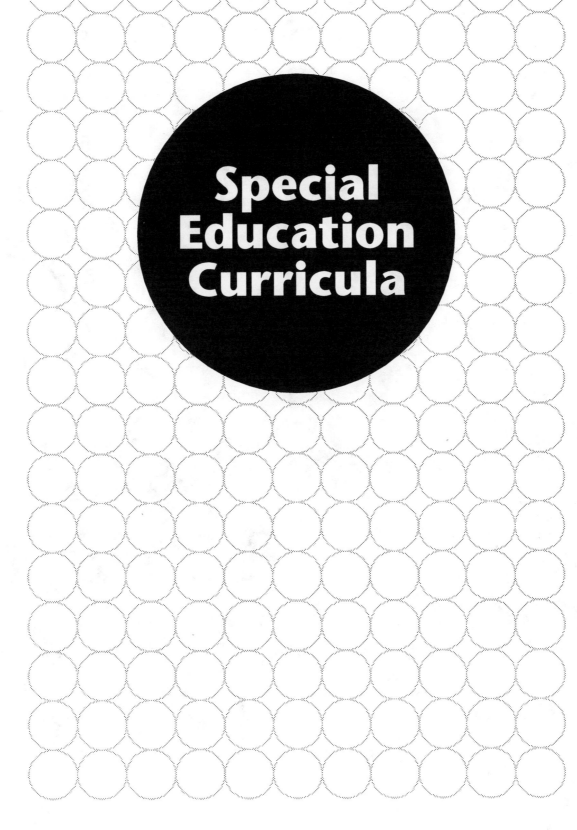

Special Education Curricula

Changes in You

Title: *Changes in You: The Curriculum—
An Introduction to Sexuality Education
Through an Understanding of Puberty*
Author: Peggy Siegel
Year Developed: 1991
Latest Revision: None
Target Grade Level: Grades 4 through 9
Length: 44 lessons (23 for girls, 21 for boys)
Cost: $199.00

Curriculum Description

Curriculum Focus

The primary goal of the curriculum is to give children the knowledge and skill to help them live healthy and happy lives. It is important to provide students with straightforward information regarding the physical, social and emotional changes of puberty. Discussion of feelings, appropriate social behavior, hygiene, decision making and sexual abuse prevention are included. Emphasis is placed on maintaining a positive tone. Positive messages can serve as a strong foundation for developing responsible sexual behavior, sexual abuse prevention, teen pregnancy prevention and HIV/AIDS prevention education. Separate sex classes are considered better for students with special needs.

Lesson Format

The program is divided into separate sections for boys and girls. The last lesson in each section provides information about the other sex. Each lesson includes strategies to supplement the use of picture cards. Student level of understanding must be tested (pre/post) so that teachers can assess the areas of needed study and/or review. Reteaching is a suggested option. Student books contain picture card information and serve four purposes:

- Allow for class lessons to be reviewed for homework and to make parents aware of lesson content.
- Allow for individualized instruction between teacher and student.

Changes in You *(continued)*

- Allow for additional study time.
- Reinforce learning by enabling the student to follow along in the book during the lesson.

Lesson outlines include objectives, vocabulary and procedure.

Package Contents

Includes tests (A, B and C) appropriate for three levels of impairment. Also includes student books, parent guide books, a letter to parents and an index of picture cards. The appendix contains numbered and labeled worksheets.

Publisher Information

James Stanfield Publishing Company, P.O. Box 41058, Santa Barbara, California 93140; (800) 421-6534 or (805) 897-1185.

Family Education Program

Title: *The Family Education Program*
Author: Planned Parenthood: Shasta-Diablo
Year Developed: 1990
Latest Revision: None
Target Grade Level: Special populations
Length: 14 sessions
Cost: $35.00

Curriculum Description

Curriculum Format

This curriculum does not promote sexual activity. The goal of the program is to provide accurate information about sexuality and responsible decision making. Fostering positive self-esteem and assertiveness skills will empower students to react effectively in dangerous situations. A positive approach in teaching students with disabilities is critical because many children with special needs are given very negative messages about their sexuality and are often socialized to be vulnerable. Development of appropriate "life skills" is a primary focus of the curriculum.

Lesson Format

Each session is outlined as follows:
- Goals.
- Materials.
- Key words.
- Getting started—includes review questions and questions to ask related to the lesson.
- Review.
- Closure.

The program is broken down into two units; one unit is designed for the developmentally disabled student. In each of the Getting Started sections of the unit a familiar set of structured activities are repeated in sequence:
- Wearing of name tags.
- Chanting of familiar learned "phrases" and practice "noises" with applause when appropriate.

- Breathing exercises.
- Joining hands (optional).
- Review.

The unit designed for the emotionally and learning disabled differs in structure. Each session includes goals, materials, introduction and review, content and closure. All lessons include the use of name tags and question boxes.

Package Contents

An appendix includes the following:
- Class handout for reproduction.
- Teacher training outline with handouts and exercises for training in teaching this curriculum.
- A materials section which includes (1) black and white drawings that can be reproduced in transparency form, (2) a listing of materials that can be made or found (pictures, photos), and (3) a listing of sources to order life-size dolls, life-size drawings and suggested videos.
- A resource guide for parents and professionals.
- "Key Issues" which gives additional background information that is topic-specific.
- Evaluation—pre/post test, along with an evaluation timeline.

Publisher Information

Planned Parenthood: Shasta-Diablo, 2185 Pacheco Street, Concord, California 94520; (510) 676-0505.

F.L.A.S.H. Special Ed.

Title: *Special Education: Secondary F.L.A.S.H.*
(Family Life and Sexual Health)
Author: Jane Strangle
Year Developed: 1991
Latest Revision: None
Target Grade Level: Grades 7 through 12
Length: 28 lessons, divided into 9 sections
Cost: $40.00

Curriculum Description

Curriculum Focus

The curriculum is designed for use in special education classrooms to provide teachers with tools for students with diverse learning challenges. The curriculum is based on "universal" values:

- Respect must be given for the individuality of the student and his or her peers in the classroom.
- Honest communication is fundamental in all relationships.
- People have a responsibility to learn as much as possible about themselves and the people that they care about.

The goal is to enable individuals to become knowledgeable about human development and reproduction and to respect and appreciate themselves and others. Of particular relevance to the student with disabilities is development of adequate social skills and social support networks.

Lesson Format

This curriculum is an adaptation of 5/6, 7/8 and 9/10 F.L.A.S.H., incorporating many of the same activities and concepts. An overview gives the lesson title along with a summary of objectives for the lesson. Each lesson is outlined as follows:

- Student learning objectives.
- Materials needed.
- Agenda.
- Activity.
- Reproductive transparency masters and worksheet masters.
- Trusted adult exercises (optional).

F.L.A.S.H. Special Ed. *(continued)*

There is no suggested sequence for each lesson. Many lessons can be incorporated with other units. The "Private/Public" session and "Anatomy" sessions provide a foundation for lessons that follow; it is suggested that they be taught first and in sequence. Adaptations and options for more-challenged learners are written in the left-hand column of the lesson description.

Package Contents

A "Special Preparation" section includes information to be used by the teacher before starting the unit. This section discusses the importance of knowing state and local guidelines, and of preparing administrators, parents, materials and the teacher. In addition, worksheet and transparency masters supplement each lesson.

The appendix includes state guidelines, signs and symptoms of sexual abuse, an assessment tool (pretest) to evaluate readiness, a F.L.A.S.H. curriculum overview, bibliography, list of audiovisual suppliers and community resources.

Publisher Information

Seattle–King County Department of Public Health, Family Planning Publications, 2124 4th Avenue, Seattle, Washington 98121; (206) 296-4672.

Life Horizons

Title: *Socialization and Sex Education:*
The Life Horizons Curriculum Module
Authors: Geraldine Rouse and Carol Birch
Year Developed: 1991
Latest Revision: None
Target Grade Level: Ages 15 to 21 (not necessarily enrolled in school)
Length: 31 lessons
Cost: $399.00 each; $599.00 for both sets

Curriculum Description

Curriculum Focus

This is a comprehensive curriculum based on practices demonstrated to be effective for individuals with learning difficulties or delays. Problem-solving and language-based instruction is the underlying framework of the curriculum. An important feature of this program is the utilization of experiences meaningful to the student.

Lesson Format

Lesson plans have been coordinated with Life Horizons I and II. Each lesson contains:

- Overview for the teacher—a preview of activities that teachers should complete before presenting the lesson.
- Objectives for the teacher.
- Student objectives, written in a format that students can understand.
- Vocabulary—listed in order of appearance in the lesson.
- Instructional activities—provide information, check for understanding of concepts and provide practice.
- Closure activities—assess student attainment of goals.
- Parent contact by memo.
- Listings of additional activities.

Some lessons are identified as intended to be taught sex-segregated.

Life Horizons (continued)

Package Contents

Examples of charts and schematic mapping are included in each lesson. An appendix includes:
- Parent permission forms.
- Problem-solving charts with categorized listing by lesson.
- Bibliography.

Life Horizons I and II are media packages which contain slides and videotapes. Life Horizons I is designed to present the physical and psychological aspects of sexuality. Life Horizons II focuses mainly on the social aspects of being a complete sexual person. A teacher handbook provides a rationale and narrative for each slide presentation.

Publisher Information

James Stanfield Publishing Company, P.O. Box 41058, Santa Barbara, California 93140; (800) 421-6534 or (805) 897-1185.

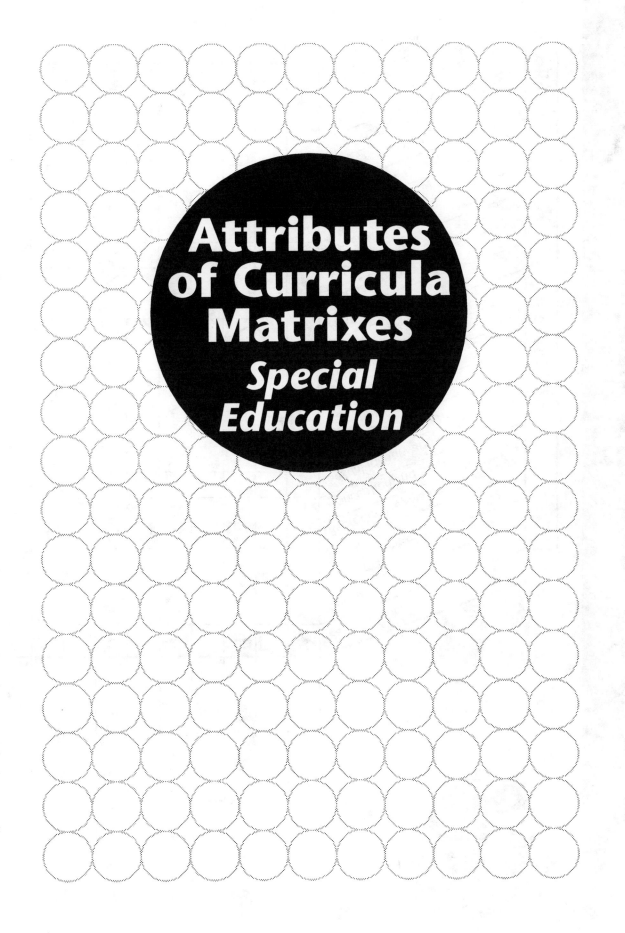

Attributes
of Curricula
Matrixes
Special
Education

Attributes of Curricula

Special Education

Curriculum	Page Number	Puberty	Body Image	Gender Roles	Reproductive Anatomy/Physiology	Conception and Birth	Sexual Identity and Orientation	Relationships	Parenting	Sexual Expression	STD Transmission	HIV Transmission	Abstinence	Pregnancy prevention	STD Prevention	HIV Prevention	Sexual Exploitation	Reproductive Health	Healthy Sexuality	Responsibility for Decisions	Abstinence (Philosophy)	Using Protection if Sexually Active	Philosophy Not Clear
					Content															Philosophy			
Changes In You (Level 2/3)	117	✓		✓						✓							✓	✓					
Family Education Program (Level 3/4)	119	✓	✓	✓	✓	✓	✓	✓	✓	✓	✓	✓	✓	✓	✓	✓	✓	✓					
F.L.A.S.H. Special Ed. (Level 3/4)	121	✓		✓	✓	✓	✓	✓	✓	✓	✓	✓	✓	✓	✓	✓	✓	✓					
Life Horizons (Level 4)	123	✓		✓	✓	✓	✓	✓	✓	✓	✓	✓	✓	✓	✓	✓	✓		✓				

(For descriptions of attributes, see p. 129.)

Curriculum

	Teaching Strategies													Skill-Building Strategies													
	Parent/Guardian Involvement	Peer Helper Component	Community Speakers/Involvement	Audiovisual Materials	Skills Practice and Rehearsal	Case Studies/Scenarios	Cooperative Learning/Small Groups	Journals/Story Writing	Student Worksheets	Large-Group Discussion	Teacher Lecture	Anonymous Question Box	Groundrules	Planning/Goal-Setting Skills	Decision-Making Skills	Conflict-Management Skills	Refusal Skills	Assertiveness Skills	General Communication Skills	Community Resources	Perceived STD/HIV Risk	Perceived Pregnancy Risk	Peer Norms	Consequences of Decisions	Influences on Decisions	Self-Awareness/Self-Esteem	Personal Values
Changes in You	✓		✓	✓	✓	✓	✓	✓		✓	✓	✓	✓			✓					✓						
Family Education Program						✓	✓				✓	✓				✓										✓	✓
F.L.A.S.H. Special Ed.	✓			✓	✓	✓	✓	✓		✓	✓	✓	✓	✓	✓	✓	✓	✓	✓	✓	✓	✓		✓	✓		✓
Life Horizons	✓			✓	✓	✓					✓	✓		✓	✓	✓	✓	✓		✓				✓			✓

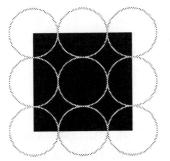

Descriptions of Attributes

Content

Puberty
Physical changes that occur in males and females during puberty; individual differences in growth rates; feelings/emotions associated with changes during puberty.

Body Image
Individual variations in size, shape, etc.; uniqueness of each person; physical appearance as determined by heredity, environment, and health habits; disabilities; portrayal of body image by media; effect of physical appearance on how people interact with others.

Gender Roles
Messages from families, friends, media and society about how males and females should behave; both genders having similar talents, characteristics, strengths, hopes and need for equal opportunities; gender role stereotypes; laws protecting the rights of men and women.

Reproductive Anatomy/Physiology
Human body has capability to reproduce; body parts have correct names and specific functions; maturation of reproductive organs occurs at puberty; hormones influence sexual and reproductive function.

Conception and Birth

Union of sperm and egg in fertilization; heredity; pregnancy and development of the fetus; genetic disorders and birth defects; stages of birth; medical procedures and new reproductive technology.

Sexual Identity and Orientation

Attraction; definition of sexual orientation, including heterosexual, homosexual and bisexual; theories about what determines sexual orientation; mistreatment and denial of rights based on sexual orientation; support services for questioning youth.

Relationships

Definition of family; types of families; roles and responsibilities of family members; friendships with people of both genders; expressing love and affection; dating; importance of honest and open communication; shared responsibility in marriage; divorce; community resources.

Parenting

Skills and information needed to make good parents; balance of parenting and full-time job; difficulties of being a teen parent; different types of parenting as children get older; raising a child with special needs.

Sexual Expression

Ways to show love and affection without having sex; natural physical response to touch; sexual response experienced differently by each person; masturbation, fantasy and shared sexual behavior; capacity to respond sexually throughout life.

STD Transmission

Causes of sexually transmitted disease; modes of transmission; signs and symptoms; long-term effects of untreated STD; importance of open communication with partner; community resources for testing, treatment and counseling; hotlines.

HIV Transmission

Type of sexually transmitted disease; caused by human immunodeficiency virus (HIV); modes of transmission; signs and symptoms; differences from other STD; community resources for testing, treatment and counseling; hotlines.

Abstinence

Safest, most effective method of preventing STD, HIV infection and pregnancy; advantages of choosing not to have sex; physical and emotional readiness for sexual intercourse; importance of open and honest communication; always having a choice; giving and receiving pleasure without having sex.

Pregnancy Prevention

Decisions to have children based on religious beliefs, personal values and cultural traditions; methods of contraception, including advantages, disadvantages and effective use; individual responsibility for getting and using protection; importance of honest and open communication with partner.

STD Prevention

Methods of STD prevention, including advantages, disadvantages and effective use; individual responsibility for getting and using protection; importance of honest and open communication with partner; community resources.

HIV Prevention

Methods of HIV infection prevention, including advantages, disadvantages and effective use; individual responsibility for getting and using protection; importance of honest and open communication with partner; community resources.

Sexual Exploitation

Sexual harassment; sexual abuse; acquaintance rape; other types of sexual exploitation; individual rights related to any type of sexual exploitation; protecting oneself, including avoiding potentially dangerous situations and learning self-defense; community resources; support services.

Reproductive Health

Individual responsibility for health; importance of cleanliness, nutrition and exercise; routine physical examination; breast self-examination; testicular self-examination; prenatal effects of smoking, drinking and using other substances; birth defects and genetic counseling.

Philosophy

Promotes Healthy Sexuality

The curriculum presents sexuality as a natural and healthy part of everyday living. It is maintained that each person expresses his or her sexuality in a variety of ways based on personal background and experience. The curriculum addresses the physical, psychological, emotional, social, ethical and spiritual dimensions of healthy sexuality.

Promotes Responsibility for Decisions

The curriculum supports each individual's right and obligation to make decisions about his or her sexuality. The curriculum empowers young people to make responsible decisions by helping them examine internal and external influences on personal decisions, recognize short- and long-term consequences of their decisions for themselves and others, and access information and services through personal support systems and community resources.

Promotes Abstinence

The curriculum presents abstinence as the safest, most effective way to prevent sexually transmitted disease, HIV infection and pregnancy. It addresses the advantages of choosing not to have sexual intercourse, the benefits of delaying sex, and the risks of having sex if a person is not ready or does not want to.

Promotes Using Protection If Sexually Active

The curriculum acknowledges that some young people will have sexual intercourse and presents methods of protection from sexually transmitted disease, HIV infection and pregnancy. It discusses advantages, disadvantages and effectiveness of these methods.

Philosophy Not Clear

The curriculum has no clear focus.

Skill-Building Strategies

Examining Personal Values
The curriculum includes activities that help young people identify what they believe, what they think is important, and how personal values affect their sexuality-related decisions.

Increasing Self-Awareness/Building Self-Esteem
The curriculum includes activities that help young people become aware of their likes and dislikes, capabilities and limitations, talents and skills; appreciate their own uniqueness; and accept individual differences.

Examining Influences on Decisions
The curriculum includes activities that focus on the internal influences (wanting to be accepted, be part of a group, take risks, feel normal, feel good, etc.) and external influences (parents/caregivers, other adults, peers, media) that affect sexuality-related decisions.

Identifying Consequences of Decisions
The curriculum includes activities that help young people look at short- and long-term physical, emotional, social and legal consequences of sexuality-related decisions for themselves and others.

Addressing Peer Norms
The curriculum includes activities that allow young people to share their perceptions of norms related to abstinence and use of protection, and that promote changes in the normative message (e.g., making posters and pamphlets to support the message that "not everyone is doing it").

Examining Perceived Pregnancy Risk
The curriculum includes activities to help young people examine the risk of getting pregnant (based on specific behaviors) and understand how they can change their behaviors to decrease the probability of pregnancy.

Examining Perceived STD/HIV Risk
The curriculum includes activities to help young people examine the risk of getting a sexually transmitted disease, including HIV, and understand how they can change their behaviors to reduce the risk of becoming infected with STD/HIV.

Accessing Community Resources

The curriculum includes activities that help young people identify sources of information and services in the community, including community agencies, hotlines, clinics and support groups.

Building General Communication Skills

The curriculum includes activities where young people learn to communicate clearly—verbally and nonverbally; to listen actively; and to express their thoughts, feelings, attitudes, beliefs, values and ideas about sexuality-related issues.

Building Assertiveness Skills

The curriculum includes activities that give young people practice in saying what they think and standing up for what they believe, without hurting or denying the rights of others. It also helps students understand the differences between passive, assertive and aggressive responses.

Building Refusal Skills

The curriculum includes activities that help young people practice effective ways to say "no" without jeopardizing their peer and family relationships.

Building Conflict-Management Skills

The curriculum includes activities that help young people solve problems and resolve conflicts in relationships without using guilt, anger and/or intimidation. It also provides opportunities to practice negotiation skills.

Building Decision-Making Skills

The curriculum includes activities that help young people examine real-life situations, generate possible solutions, and anticipate the short- and long-term consequences of having sex and having unprotected sex, as well as understand how each decision can affect subsequent decisions.

Building Planning/Goal-Setting Skills

The curriculum includes activities that help young people examine personal expectations and those of others, identify short- and long-term personal goals, and identify barriers to achieving their personal goals. It also provides opportunities to use planning skills in situations related to having sex or having unprotected sex.

134

Teaching Strategies

Groundrules

With student input, the teacher establishes groundrules for classroom discussion of sexuality-related issues.

Anonymous Question Box

An anonymous question box is set up so that students can ask questions or express feelings and concerns without fear of embarrassment.

Teacher Lecture

The teacher provides key information directly to students with a minimum of class participation and interruption.

Large-Group Discussion

In an open discussion involving the entire class, students are guided by the teacher to share ideas, thoughts and beliefs about a sexuality-related issue.

Student Worksheets

A variety of written questions or forms are used to help students focus on particular topics. This strategy allows the sharing of opinions and ideas without having to discuss them openly with the rest of the class.

Journals/Story Writing

Students are given opportunities to write their thoughts and feelings about the sexuality-related issues discussed in class in personal journals or diaries.

Cooperative Learning/Small Groups

Lessons include small-group discussions about sexuality-related issues. Students are assigned certain roles and responsibilities within the group.

Case Studies/Scenarios

Lessons include case studies and real-life scenarios to help students practice personal and social skills.

Skills Practice and Rehearsal

Students are given a variety of opportunities to practice newly learned personal and social skills, including roleplays, small-group activities and worksheets.

Audiovisual Materials

The teacher uses audiovisual materials when presenting information and/or skills (transparencies, videos, slides, films, etc.).

Community Speakers/Involvement

Outside speakers from community agencies are asked to present sexuality-related information or skills.

Peer Helper Component

Same-age or cross-age peers are used in the presentation of sexuality-related information or skills.

Parent/Guardian Involvement

Homework assignments and curriculum activities are designed to be completed by parents or caregivers and their children.

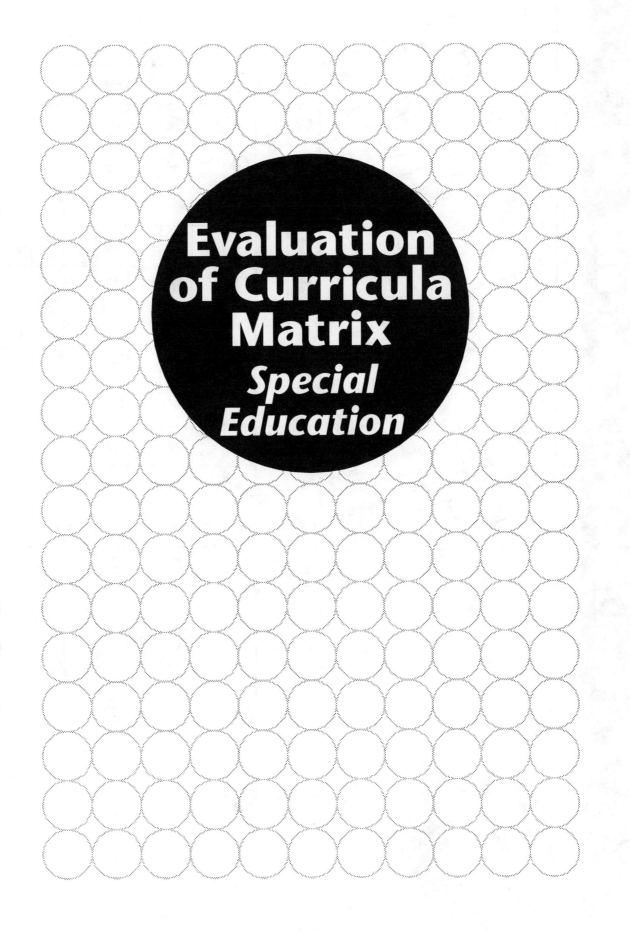

Evaluation
of Curricula
Matrix
Special
Education

Evaluation of Curricula

Special Education

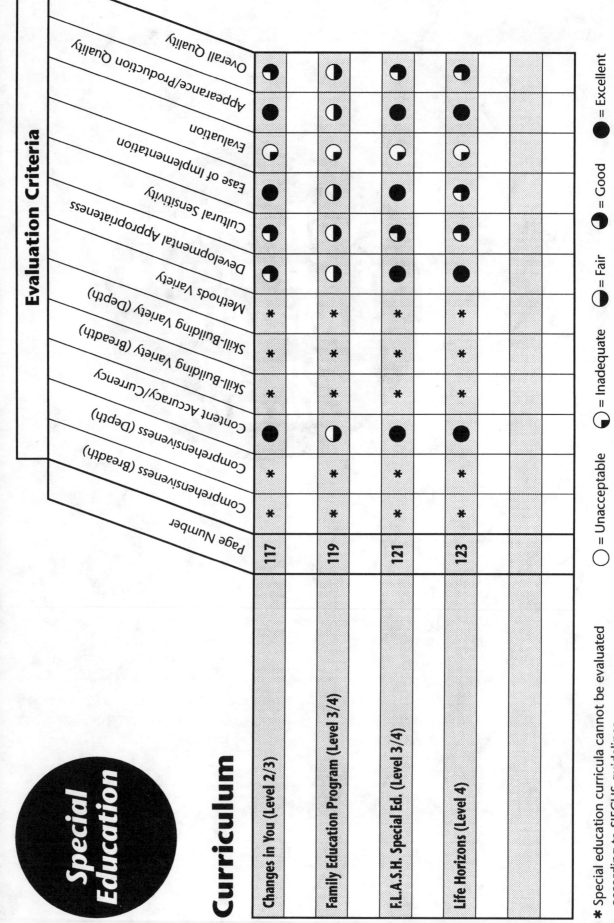

Evaluation Criteria (columns): Page Number · Comprehensiveness (Breadth) · Comprehensiveness (Depth) · Content Accuracy/Currency · Skill-Building Variety (Breadth) · Skill-Building Variety (Depth) · Methods Variety · Developmental Appropriateness · Cultural Sensitivity · Ease of Implementation · Evaluation · Appearance/Production Quality · Overall Quality

Curriculum (rows):

Curriculum	Page Number
Changes in You (Level 2/3)	117
Family Education Program (Level 3/4)	119
F.L.A.S.H. Special Ed. (Level 3/4)	121
Life Horizons (Level 4)	123

Legend:
○ = Unacceptable   ◔ = Inadequate   ◑ = Fair   ◕ = Good   ● = Excellent

* Special education curricula cannot be evaluated according to SIECUS guidelines.

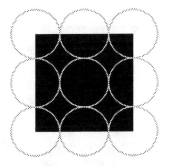

Descriptions of Evaluation Criteria

Evaluation Criteria

Comprehensiveness (Breadth)
The curriculum includes *all* developmentally appropriate key concepts as described by the *Guidelines for Comprehensive Sexuality Education* (National Guidelines Task Force, 1991).

Comprehensiveness (Depth)
The curriculum includes *all* subconcepts and developmental messages within each key concept as described by the *Guidelines for Comprehensive Sexuality Education* (National Guidelines Task Force, 1991).

Content Accuracy/Currency
The curriculum provides accurate information about sexuality-related topics and is based on current research and theory. Graphs, charts and tables are current and representative of the target population.

The curriculum is up to date and presents information in ways that interest today's young people. Graphs, charts, language and pictures reflect current issues and trends.

Skill-Building Variety (Breadth)

The curriculum provides activities to build a variety of personal and social skills: decision-making, general communication, assertiveness, refusal, conflict management and planning/goal-setting skills.

Skill-Building Variety (Depth)

The curriculum addresses each personal and social skill comprehensively: the skill is introduced focusing on its importance; steps for skill development are presented; the skill is modeled for students; the skill is practiced and rehearsed with a variety of situations; and feedback/reinforcement is provided.

Methods Variety

To meet the diverse needs and learning styles of students, the curriculum provides a variety of instructional strategies for providing key information; encouraging creative expression; sharing thoughts, feelings and opinions; and developing critical thinking skills.

Developmental Appropriateness

The curriculum presents sexuality-related information, instructional strategies, and personal and social skills appropriate for the cognitive, emotional and social developmental level and personal experience of the targeted grades. Lessons are adaptable to individual student needs.

Cultural Sensitivity

The curriculum does not contain information or activities that are biased in terms of race or ethnicity, sex or gender roles, family types, sexual orientation, and/or age. It portrays a variety of social groups and lifestyles in its examples, pictures and descriptions. Instructional strategies take into account the cultural and ethnic values, customs and practices of the community.

Ease of Implementation

The curriculum includes features that make it "user friendly." That is, all materials and master copies necessary for implementation are included; it is well organized, with clear, thorough instructions; it can easily be updated; and it provides references and support materials for teachers.

Evaluation

The curriculum provides methods for evaluating levels of student knowledge, attitudes and/or skills that are consistent with curriculum goals and lesson objectives.

Appearance/Production Quality

The curriculum is clearly written, up to date, aesthetically pleasing (including print quality), and likely to elicit student interest.

Overall Quality

Overall assessment of the quality of the curriculum is based on scores in comprehensiveness, content accuracy/currency, skill-building variety, methods variety, developmental appropriateness, cultural sensitivity, ease of implementation, evaluation and appearance/production quality.

Appendix A

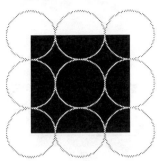

Evaluation Matrixes and Worksheet

For each of the criteria listed, rate the curriculum according to the following scale: 0 = unacceptable; 1 = inadequate; 2 = fair; 3 = good; and 4 = excellent.

Evaluation Criteria 1 and 2: Comprehensiveness (Breadth and Depth)

Definition: The curriculum includes *all* developmentally appropriate key concepts (breadth) and *all* subconcepts and developmental messages within each key concept (depth) as described by the SIECUS *Guidelines for Comprehensive Sexuality Education*. (Review the attributes of curricula matrix to determine breadth of content addressed.)

☐ Includes *all* developmentally appropriate key concepts (breadth)

Comments/references to areas of concern:

_____

_____

_____

_____

143

☐ Includes *all* subconcepts and developmental messages within each key concept (depth)

Comments/references to areas of concern:

_____

_____

_____

_____

Evaluation Criteria 3:
Content Accuracy/Currency

Definition: The curriculum provides accurate information about sexuality-related topics and is based on current research and theory. Graphs, charts and tables are current and representative of the target population (accuracy). The curriculum is up to date and presents information in ways that interest today's young people. Graphs, charts, language and pictures reflect current issues and trends (currency).

☐ Information is scientifically accurate

Comments/references to areas of concern:

_____

_____

_____

_____

☐ Information is based on current research and theory

Comments/references to areas of concern:

_____

_____

_____

_____

☐ Graphs, charts, and tables are current
Comments/references to areas of concern:

_____
_____
_____
_____

☐ Graphs, charts, and tables represent target population
Comments/references to areas of concern:

_____
_____
_____
_____

☐ Information is up-to-date
Comments/references to areas of concern:

_____
_____
_____
_____

☐ Information interesting to today's young people
Comments/references to areas of concern:

_____
_____
_____
_____

☐ Graphs, charts, language, pictures reflect current issues
Comments/references to areas of concern:

_____
_____
_____

Evaluation Criteria 4 & 5:
Skill-Building Variety (Breadth and Depth)

Definition: The curriculum provides activities to build a variety of personal and social skills: decision-making, general communication, assertiveness, refusal, conflict management, and planning/goal-setting skills (breadth). It addresses each skill comprehensively: the skill is introduced focusing on its importance, steps for skill development are presented, the skill is modeled for students, the skill is practiced and rehearsed, and feedback/reinforcement is provided (depth). (Review the attributes of curricula matrix to determine breadth of skills addressed.)

☐ Variety of personal and social skills presented (breadth)
   Comments/references to areas of concern:

   _____

   _____

   _____

   _____

☐ Skills are addressed comprehensively (depth)
   Comments/references to areas of concern:

   _____

   _____

   _____

   _____

☐ Skills are practiced and rehearsed to develop student competency
   Comments/references to areas of concern:

   _____

   _____

   _____

   _____

Evaluation Matrixes and Worksheet

Evaluation Criteria 6: Methods Variety

Definition: To meet the diverse needs and learning styles of students, the curriculum provides a variety of instructional strategies for providing key information; encouraging creative expression; sharing thoughts, feelings and opinions; and developing critical thinking skills.

☐ Includes variety of strategies for providing information
Comments/references to areas of concern:

_____

_____

_____

_____

☐ Includes strategies encouraging creative expression
Comments/references to areas of concern:

_____

_____

_____

_____

☐ Includes strategies for sharing thoughts, feelings, opinions
Comments/references to areas of concern:

_____

_____

_____

_____

☐ Includes strategies for developing critical thinking skills
Comments/references to areas of concern:

_____

_____

_____

_____

Sexuality Education Curricula: The Consumer's Guide

Evaluation Criteria 7: Developmental Appropriateness

Definition: The curriculum presents sexuality-related information, instructional strategies, and personal and social skills appropriate for the cognitive, emotional and social developmental level and personal experience of the targeted grades. Lessons are adaptable to individual student needs.

☐ Content and skills are reinforced and built upon

Comments/references to areas of concern:

_____

_____

_____

_____

☐ Content is appropriate for target grade levels

Comments/reference to areas of concern:

_____

_____

_____

_____

☐ Skills are appropriate for target grade levels

Comments/references to areas of concern:

_____

_____

_____

_____

☐ Instructional strategies are appropriate for target grade levels
Comments/references to areas of concern:

_____

_____

_____

_____

☐ Student activities are appropriate for target grade levels
Comments/references to areas of concern:

_____

_____

_____

_____

☐ Materials can be adapted to meet individual student needs
Comments/references to areas of concern:

_____

_____

_____

_____

Evaluation Criteria 8: Cultural Sensitivity

Definition: The curriculum does not contain information or activities that are biased in terms of race or ethnicity, sex or gender roles, family types, sexual orientation, and/or age. It portrays a variety of social groups and lifestyles in its examples, pictures and descriptions. Instructional strategies take into account the cultural and ethnic values, customs and practices of the community.

☐ No stereotypic references re: gender
Comments/references to areas of concern:

_____

_____

_____

_____

☐ No stereotypic references re: race/ethnicity
Comments/references to areas of concern:

_____

_____

_____

_____

☐ No stereotypic references re: family types
Comments/references to areas of concern:

_____

_____

_____

_____

☐ No stereotypic references re: sexual orientation
Comments/references to areas of concern:

_____

_____

_____

_____

☐ No stereotypic references re: age
Comments/references to areas of concern:

_____

_____

_____

_____

☐ Portrays a wide variety of social groups and lifestyles in examples, pictures, and descriptions
Comments/references to areas of concern:

_____

_____

_____

_____

☐ Takes into account the cultural and ethnic values, customs, and practices of the community
Comments/references to areas of concern:

_____

_____

_____

_____

Evaluation Criteria 9: Ease of Implementation

Definition: The curriculum includes features that make it "user friendly." That is, all materials and master copies necessary for implementation are included; it is well organized, with clear, thorough instructions; it can easily be updated; and it provides references and support materials for teachers.

☐ Includes all materials and master copies necessary for implementation

Comments/references to areas of concern:

_____

_____

_____

_____

☐ Well organized with clear, thorough instructions

Comments/references to areas of concern:

_____

_____

_____

_____

☐ Easily updated

Comments/references to areas of concern:

_____

_____

_____

_____

☐ Provides references and support materials for teachers

Comments/references to areas of concern:

_____

_____

_____

_____

☐ Does not require special training for implementation

Comments/references to areas of concern:

_____

_____

_____

_____

Evaluation Criteria 10: Evaluation

Definition: The curriculum provides methods for evaluating levels of student knowledge, attitudes and/or skills that are consistent with curriculum goals and lesson objectives.

☐ Provides evaluation/assessment instruments or activities re: student knowledge

Comments/references to areas of concern:

_____

_____

_____

_____

☐ Provides evaluation/assessment instruments or activities re: student attitudes

Comments/references to areas of concern:

_____

_____

_____

_____

☐ Provides evaluation/assessment instruments or activities re: student skills

Comments/references to areas of concern:

_____

_____

_____

_____

☐ Evaluation instruments or activities are clearly linked to curriculum objectives

Comments/references to areas of concern:

_____

_____

_____

_____

Evaluation Criteria 11: Appearance/Production Quality

The curriculum is clearly written, up to date, aesthetically pleasing (including print quality), and likely to elicit student interest.

☐ Written in a clear, readable style

Comments/references to areas of concern:

_____

_____

_____

_____

☐ Printed in high quality type on good paper

Comments/references to areas of concern:

_____

_____

_____

_____

154

☐ Materials are aesthetically pleasing
Comments/references to areas of concern:

_____

_____

_____

_____

☐ Uses graphics, language, and design appropriate for current times
Comments/references to areas of concern:

_____

_____

_____

_____

Attributes of Curricula

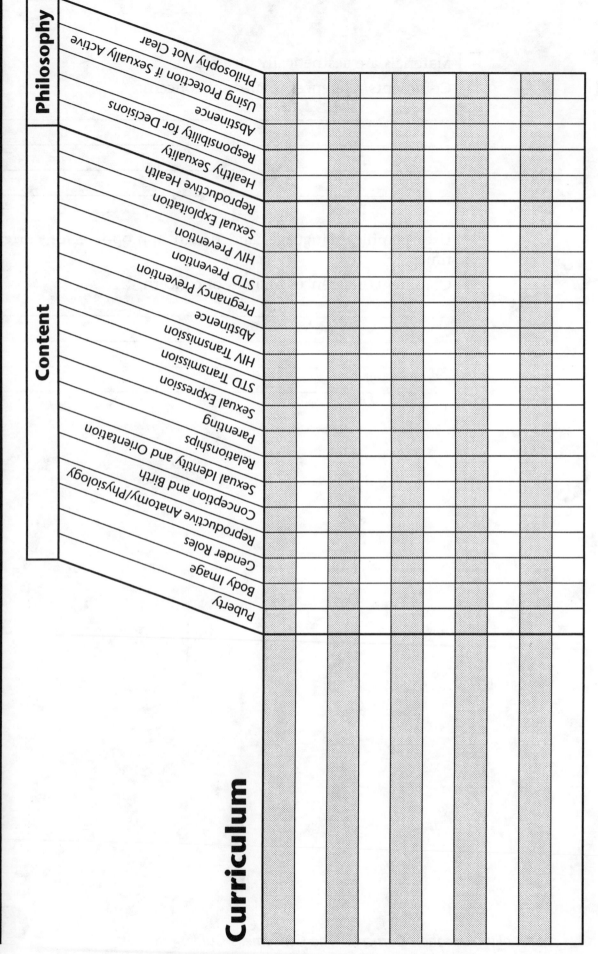

	Philosophy			Content																			
Curriculum	Philosophy Not Clear	Using Protection if Sexually Active	Abstinence	Responsibility for Decisions	Healthy Sexuality	Reproductive Health	Sexual Exploitation	HIV Prevention	STD Prevention	Pregnancy Prevention	Abstinence	HIV Transmission	STD Transmission	Sexual Expression	Parenting	Relationships	Sexual Identity and Orientation	Conception and Birth	Reproductive Anatomy/Physiology	Gender Roles	Body Image	Puberty		

Teaching Strategies

- Parent/Guardian Involvement
- Peer Helper Component
- Community Speakers/Involvement
- Audiovisual Materials
- Skills Practice and Rehearsal
- Case Studies/Scenarios
- Cooperative Learning/Small Groups
- Journals/Story Writing
- Student Worksheets
- Large-Group Discussion
- Teacher Lecture
- Anonymous Question Box

Skill-Building Strategies

- Groundrules
- Planning/Goal-Setting Skills
- Decision-Making Skills
- Conflict-Management Skills
- Refusal Skills
- Assertiveness Skills
- General Communication Skills
- Community Resources
- Perceived STD/HIV Risk
- Perceived Pregnancy Risk
- Peer Norms
- Consequences of Decisions
- Influences on Decisions
- Self-Awareness/Self-Esteem
- Personal Values

Curriculum

Evaluation of Curricula

Evaluation Criteria

Curriculum	Comprehensiveness (Breadth)	Comprehensiveness (Depth)	Content Accuracy/Currency	Skill-Building Variety (Breadth)	Skill-Building Variety (Depth)	Methods Variety	Developmental Appropriateness	Cultural Sensitivity	Ease of Implementation	Evaluation	Appearance/Production Quality	Overall Quality

0 = Unacceptable   1 = Inadequate   2 = Fair   3 = Good   4 = Excellent

Appendix B

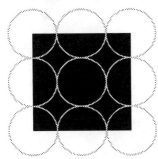

Programs Not Included in *The Consumer's Guide*

TITLE: *Bodies, Birth and Babies: Sexuality Education in Early Childhood Programs*
AUTHORS: Peggy Brick, Nan Davis, Maxine Fischel, Trudie Lupo, Jean Marshall and Ann MacVicar
PUBLISHER INFORMATION: The Center for Family Life Education, Planned Parenthood of Greater Northern New Jersey, Inc., 575 Main Street, Hackensack, New Jersey 07601; (201) 489-1265
REASON FOR EXCLUSION: Not a school-based curriculum

TITLE: *Chances or Choices*
AUTHOR: Dobie Bielka
PUBLISHER INFORMATION: Planned Parenthood of Seattle–King County, 2211 East Madison, Seattle, Washington 98112; (206) 328-7715
REASON FOR EXCLUSION: Not a sexuality education curriculum

TITLES: *Choices: A Teen Woman's Journal for Self-awareness and Personal Planning* and *Challenges: A Young Man's Journal for Self-awareness and Personal Planning*
AUTHORS: Mindy Bingham, Judy Edmondson, Sue Fajen, Michele Jackman and Sandy Stryker (*Choices*); Mindy Bingham, Judy Edmondson and Sandy Stryker (*Challenges*)
PUBLISHER INFORMATION: Advocacy Press, Box 236, Santa Barbara, California 93102; (805) 962-2728
REASON FOR EXCLUSION: Not a school-based curriculum

TITLE: *Cultural Pride*
(Latino Family Life Education Curriculum Series)
AUTHOR: Ana Consuelo Matiella
PUBLISHER INFORMATION: ETR Associates, P.O. Box 1830, Santa Cruz, California 95061-1830; (800) 321-4407
REASON FOR EXCLUSION: Written for one special population

TITLE: *The Dynamics of Relationships: A Guide for Developing Self-Esteem and Social Skills for Teens and Young Adults*
AUTHOR: Patricia Kramer
PUBLISHER INFORMATION: Equal Partners, 3371 Beaverwood Lane, Silver Springs, Maryland 20906; (301) 871-9665
REASON FOR EXCLUSION: Not a curriculum

TITLE: *Family Life Education: Curriculum Guide*
AUTHOR: Steven Bignell
PUBLISHER INFORMATION: ETR Associates, P.O. Box 1830, Santa Cruz, California 95061-1830; (800) 321-4407
REASON FOR EXCLUSION: Not a curriculum

TITLE: *Family Life Education: Resources for the Elementary Classroom*
AUTHORS: Lynne Ann Despelder and Albert Lee Strickland
PUBLISHER INFORMATION: ETR Associates, P.O. Box 1830, Santa Cruz, California 95061-1830; (800) 321-4407
REASON FOR EXCLUSION: Out of date; not a curriculum

TITLE: *Family Life Education: Teacher Training Manual*
AUTHORS: Ellen Wagman and Lynne Cooper
PUBLISHER INFORMATION: ETR Associates, P.O. Box 1830, Santa Cruz, California 95061-1830; (800) 321-4407
REASON FOR EXCLUSION: Not a curriculum

TITLE: *Growing Together: A Sexuality Education Program for Girls Ages 9–11.* (Part One of the series Preventing Adolescent Pregnancy Program)
AUTHORS: Girls Clubs of America, Inc.
PUBLISHER INFORMATION: Girls Incorporated, 30 East 33rd Street, New York, New York 10016; (212) 689-3700
REASON FOR EXCLUSION: Not a school-based curriculum

TITLE: *How to Be a Trainer: A Self-Instructional Manual for Training in Sexual and Reproductive Health Care*
AUTHOR: Terry Beresford
PUBLISHER INFORMATION: Planned Parenthood of Maryland, 610 North Howard Street, Baltimore, Maryland 21201; (410) 576-1400
REASON FOR EXCLUSION: Not a school-based curriculum

TITLE: *Intimacy Is for Everyone: Sex Educator's Guide to Teaching Intimacy Skills*
AUTHORS: Bob McDermott and Barbara Petrich
PUBLISHERS INFORMATION: Planned Parenthood of Santa Barbara, Inc., 518 Garden Street, Santa Barbara, California 93101; (805) 963-5801
REASON FOR EXCLUSION: Not a school-based curriculum

TITLE: *Keeping Healthy, Keeping Safe: HIV Prevention and Education Program*
AUTHORS: Girls Incorporated
PUBLISHER INFORMATION: Girls Incorporated, 30 East 33rd Street, New York, New York 10016; (212) 689-3700
REASON FOR EXCLUSION: Not a school-based curriculum; HIV specific

TITLE: *La Comunicación*
(Latino Family Life Education Curriculum Series)
AUTHOR: Gene T. Chavez
PUBLISHER INFORMATION: ETR Associates, P.O. Box 1830, Santa Cruz, California 95061-1830; (800) 321-4407
REASON FOR EXCLUSION: Written for one special population

TITLE: *La Familia*
(Latino Family Life Education Curriculum Series)
AUTHOR: Ana Consuelo Matiella
PUBLISHER INFORMATION: ETR Associates, P.O. Box 1830, Santa Cruz, California 95061-1830; (800) 321-4407
REASON FOR EXCLUSION: Written for one special population

TITLE: *La Sexualidad*
(Latino Family Life Education Curriculum Series)
AUTHOR: Elizabeth Raptis Picco
PUBLISHER INFORMATION: ETR Associates, P.O. Box 1830, Santa Cruz, California 95061-1830; (800) 321-4407
REASON FOR EXCLUSION: Written for one special population

TITLE: *Me, My World, My Future*
AUTHORS: Nancy Roach and Leanna Benn
PUBLISHER INFORMATION: Teen Aid Inc., 723 East Jackson, Spokane, Washington 99207; (509) 482-2868
REASON FOR EXCLUSION: Publisher would not allow independent review

TITLE: *Mutual Caring, Mutual Sharing: A Sexuality Education Unit for Adolescents*
AUTHOR: Cooper Thompson
PUBLISHER INFORMATION: The Strafford County Prenatal and Family Planning Program, The Clinic, P.O. Box 797, Dover, New Hampshire 03820; (603) 749-2346
REASON FOR EXCLUSION: Not a curriculum; a teacher's guide

TITLE: *New Methods for Puberty Education, Grades 4–9*
AUTHORS: Carolyn Cooperman and Chuck Rhoades
PUBLISHER INFORMATION: Center for Family Life Education, Planned Parenthood of Northern New Jersey, 575 Main Street, Hackensack, New Jersey 07601; (201) 489-1265
REASON FOR EXCLUSION: Not a curriculum

TITLE: Preventing Adolescent Pregnancy—*Health Bridge: A Collaborative Model for Delivering Health Services to Young Women Ages 12–18*
AUTHOR: Girls Incorporated
PUBLISHER INFORMATION: Girls Incorporated, 30 East 33rd Street, New York, New York 10016; 689-3700
REASON FOR EXCLUSION: Not a school-based curriculum

TITLE: *Project Plain Talk: Sexuality and Faith*
AUTHORS: Planned Parenthood Centers of West Michigan, Inc.
PUBLISHER INFORMATION: Planned Parenthood Centers of West Michigan, Inc., 425 Cherry SE, Grand Rapids, MI 49503; (616) 774-7005
REASON FOR EXCLUSION: Not a school-based curriculum

TITLE: *Saying "No" to Sex: Assertiveness and Refusal Skills Training*
AUTHOR: Mary Ellen Marmaduke
PUBLISHER INFORMATION: Saying "No" to Sex Curriculum, 2760 NW Quimby Street, Portland, Oregon 97210; (503) 227-4858, fax (503) 226-6000
REASON FOR EXCLUSION: No publisher

TITLE: *Self-Discovery—Caring, Loving and Sexuality: Using Skills to Make Tough Choices*
AUTHORS: Gilda Gussin, Ann Buxbaum and Nicholas Danforth
PUBLISHER INFORMATION: ETR Associates, P.O. Box 1830, Santa Cruz, California 95061-1830; (800) 321-4407
REASON FOR EXCLUSION: Not a curriculum

TITLE: *Sex Education for the 90's: A Practical Teacher's Guide*
AUTHOR: Kathy Lipscomb Bridge
PUBLISHER INFORMATION: J. Weston Walch, Publisher, 321 Valley Street, Box 658, Portland, Maine 04104; (207) 772-2846, fax (207) 772-3105
REASON FOR EXCLUSION: Not a school-based curriculum

TITLE: *Sex Education: Teacher's Guide and Resource Manual,* Revised Edition
AUTHOR: Steven Bignell
PUBLISHER INFORMATION: ETR Associates, P.O. Box 1830, Santa Cruz, California 95061-1830; (800) 321-4407
REASON FOR EXCLUSION: Not a curriculum

TITLE: *Sex Respect: The Option of True Sexual Freedom*
AUTHOR: Coleen Kelly Mast
PUBLISHER INFORMATION: Project Respect, Box 97, Golf, Illinois 60029; (708) 729-3308
REASON: Publisher not willing to participate

TITLE: *Sexual Commitment and Family*
AUTHORS: Steve Potter and Nancy Potter
PUBLISHER INFORMATION: Teen Aid Inc., 723 East Jackson, Spokane, Washington 99207; (509) 482-2868
REASON FOR EXCLUSION: Publisher would not allow independent review

TITLE: *STARS—Students Talking About Responsible Sexuality*
AUTHORS: Teen Empowerment Program, Planned Parenthood of Maryland
PUBLISHER INFORMATION: Planned Parenthood of Maryland, 610 North Howard Street, Baltimore, Maryland 21201; (410) 576-1400
REASON FOR EXCLUSION: Not a school-based curriculum

TITLE: *Steps Towards Adolescence*
AUTHORS: Planned Parenthood Southeastern Pennsylvania
PUBLISHER INFORMATION: Education Department, Planned Parenthood Southeastern Pennsylvania, 1144 Locust Street, Philadelphia, Pennsylvania 19107; (215) 351-5500
REASON FOR EXCLUSION: Not a school-based curriculum

TITLE: *Taking Care of Business: A Sexuality and Career Exploration Program for Young Women Ages 15–18.* (Part Three of the series Preventing Adolescent Pregnancy)
AUTHORS: Girls Clubs of America, Inc.
PUBLISHER INFORMATION: Girls Incorporated, 30 East 33rd Street, New York, New York 10016; (212) 689-3700
REASON FOR EXCLUSION: Not a school-based curriculum

TITLE: *Tomorrow's Partners, Tomorrow's Parents: A Guide for Planning Effective Family Life Education Programs*
AUTHORS: Girls Clubs of America, Inc.
PUBLISHER INFORMATION: Girls Incorporated, 30 East 33rd Street, New York, New York 10016; (212) 689-3700
REASON FOR EXCLUSION: Not a curriculum

TITLE: *Will Power/Won't Power: A Sexuality Education Program for Girls Age 12–14.* (Part Two of the series Preventing Adolescent Pregnancy)
AUTHORS: Girls Clubs of America, Inc.
PUBLISHER INFORMATION: Girls Incorporated, 30 East 33rd Street, New York, New York 10016; (212) 689-3700
REASON FOR EXCLUSION: Not a school-based curriculum

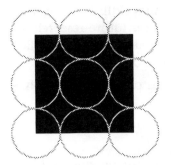

References

Alcohol, Drug Abuse, and Mental Health Administration, U.S. Public Health Service, Department of Health and Human Services. 1990. *Stopping alcohol and other drug use before it starts: The future of prevention.* Rockville, MD: Office for Substance Abuse Prevention.

Association for Sexuality Education and Training. n.d. *What criteria can be used to assess sexuality (or HIV/AIDS) curricula.* Oak Harbor, WA.

Bell, C. S., and R. J. Battjes, eds. 1987. *Prevention research: Deterring drug abuse among children and adolescents.* (NIDA Research Monograph 63: DHHS Publication No. ADM87-1334). Rockville, MD: National Institute on Drug Abuse.

Botvin, G. J., and T. A. Wills. 1985. Personal and social skills training: Cognitive-behavioral approaches to substance use prevention. In *Prevention research: Deterring drug use among children and adolescents,* ed. C. Bell and R. Battjes, 8–49. Rockville, MD: National Institute on Drug Abuse.

Cassidy, D. C., ed. 1990. *Family life education curriculum guidelines.* Minneapolis, MN: National Council on Family Relations.

Eisen, M., G. L. Zellman and A. L. McAllister. 1990. Evaluating the impact of a theory-based sexuality and contraceptive education program. *Family Planning Perspectives* 22 (6): 261–271.

English, J., A. Sancho, D. Lloyd-Kolkin and L. Hunter. 1990. *Criteria for comprehensive health education curricula.* Los Alamitos, CA: The Southwest Regional Educational Laboratory.

Fetro, J. 1992. *Personal and social skills: Understanding and integrating competencies across health content.* Santa Cruz, CA: ETR Associates.

Flay, B. R. 1985. What we know about the social influences approach to smoking prevention: Review and recommendations. In *Prevention research: Deterring drug use among children and adolescents,* ed. C. Bell and R. Battjes, 67–112. Rockville, MD: National Institute on Drug Abuse.

Glasgow, R. E., and K. D. McCaul. 1985. Social and personal skills training programs for smoking prevention: Critique and directions for future research. In *Prevention research: Deterring drug use among children and adolescents,* ed. C. Bell and R. Battjes, 50–66. Rockville, MD: National Institute on Drug Abuse.

Howard, M., and J. B. McCabe. 1991. Helping teenagers postpone sexual involvement. *Family Planning Perspectives* 22 (1): 21–26.

Kirby, D. 1993. Sexuality education: It can reduce unprotected intercourse. *SIECUS Report* 21 (2): 19–25.

Kirby, D., R. P. Barth, N. Leland and J. V. Fetro. 1991. Reducing the risk: The impact of a new curriculum on sexual risk-taking. *Family Planning Perspectives* 23 (6): 253–263.

Kumpfer, K. L. 1990. Prevention of alcohol and drug abuse: A critical review of risk factors and prevention strategies. In *Prevention of mental disorders, alcohol, and other drug use in children and adolescents,* ed. D. Shaffer, I. Phillips and N. B. Enzer, 309–372. Rockville, MD: Office for Substance Abuse Prevention.

Lando, H. A. 1985. The social influences approach to smoking prevention and progress toward an integrated smoking elimination strategy. In *Prevention research: Deterring drug use among children and adolescents,* ed. C. Bell and R. Battjes, 113–129. Rockville, MD: National Institute on Drug Abuse.

National Guidelines Task Force. 1991. *Guidelines for comprehensive sexuality education: Kindergarten–12th grade.* New York: Sex Information and Education Council of the United States.

Neutens, J. J., J. C. Drolet, M. L. Dushaw and W. Jubb. 1991. *Sexuality education within comprehensive school health education.* Kent, OH: American School Health Education.

Planned Parenthood Manitoba, Inc. 1989. *Family life education curriculum evaluation checklist.* Manitoba, Canada.

Rogers, T., B. Howard-Pitney and B. L. Bruce. 1990. *What works? A guide to school-based alcohol and drug abuse prevention curricula.* Palo Alto, CA: Health Promotion Resource Center, Stanford Center for Research in Disease and Prevention.

Schaps, E., R. DiBartolo, J. Moskowitz, C. Palley and S. Churgin. 1981. Primary prevention evaluation research: A review of 127 impact studies. *Journal of Drug Issues* 11:17–43.

Schinke, S. P., B. J. Blythe and L. D. Gilchrist. 1981. Cognitive-behavioral prevention of adolescent pregnancy. *Journal of Counseling Psychology* 28:451–454.

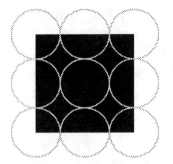

About the Authors

Christine E. Beyer, MEd, is currently working toward a PhD in health education at Southern Illinois University at Carbondale. Her masters thesis topic was "Levels of Parental Involvement and Opposition to Sex Education." She has 15 years experience as a health/sexuality educator in public schools in Illinois and Florida at the middle school, high school and university levels and has participated in curriculum development and design in comprehensive health education and sexuality education. She is also a certified Red Cross HIV/AIDS educator.

Judy C. Drolet, PhD, CHES, FASHA, received her secondary teaching credential and master's degree in health science from San Francisco State University and her doctorate in health education from the University of Oregon. She is a Certified Health Education Specialist and Fellow of the American School Health Association. She began teaching human sexuality and health education courses in 1975. Recent course emphases include sexuality education methods and issues, professional preparation, mental health, and foundations of health education. For over a decade, she has been coordinator of more than twenty graduate teaching assistants, and directed master's and doctoral student research in the Department of Health Education at Southern Illinois University at Carbondale. She has been elected to the national board of directors of the Association for the Advancement of Health Education and the American School Health Association, and national vice-president of Eta Sigma Gamma. She

Sexuality Education Curricula: The Consumer's Guide

167

received national distinguished service awards from the American School Health Association and Eta Sigma Gamma. She is coauthor of *Are You Sad Too? Helping Children Deal with Loss and Death* (ETR Associates, 1993), and coeditor of *The Sexuality Education Challenge: Promoting Healthy Sexuality in Young People* (ETR Associates, 1994).

Joyce V. Fetro, PhD, CHES, is the Acting Supervisor of School Health Programs for the San Francisco Unified School District. In that role, she is responsible for the planning and implementation of the district's comprehensive school health program. She received her doctoral degree in health education from Southern Illinois University at Carbondale with an emphasis on evaluation, instrument development and research methods. Her experience in health education spans more than twenty years, including three years as a curriculum specialist, thirteen years as a middle school teacher, two years as a university instructor, and three years conducting research and evaluation studies about the effectiveness of programs on substance use, pregnancy and HIV prevention. She is the author of *Step by Step to Substance Use Prevention: The Planner's Guide for School-Based Programs* (ETR Associates, 1991), and *Personal and Social Skills: Understanding and Integrating Competencies Across Health Content* (ETR Associates, 1992), and is coauthor of *Are You Sad Too? Helping Children Deal with Loss and Death* (ETR Associates, 1993).

Nancy L. LaCursia, MS, is currently completing the requirements for the PhD in health education at Southern Illinois University at Carbondale. Her 16 years of health education teaching experience includes the high school, college and university levels. She has taught sexuality education units within health education courses at the high school level and a family life education course at the college level and has been a copresenter at national conferences on the subject of adolescent sexual coercion. She currently serves as secretary of the Illinois Association for Professional Preparation in Health, Physical Education and Recreation.

Roberta J. Ogletree, HSD, CHES, is an assistant professor in the Department of Health Education and Recreation at Southern Illinois University. She was awarded the Health and Safety Doctorate from Indiana University in 1991. She has been a health educator for 19 years and has teaching experience at the high school, junior college and university levels. At Southern Illinois University her specialty areas are human sexuality, curriculum in health education, and women's health, and she teaches courses in those areas. An active member of the American School Health Association, she has held offices on the Sexuality Education Council and is also active in the Health Education Council the Health Educator Section and the Research Council. She has published articles dealing with sexual coercion, health counseling, and contraceptive practices of college students.

Barbara A. Rienzo, PhD, CHES, FASHA, has taught the human sexuality education professional preparation course at the University of Florida, Gainesville, since 1977. She has conducted extensive teacher inservice training throughout the southeast and Florida for the U.S. Department of Education and the State of Florida Department of Education and has written two monographs on implementing human sexuality education programs in schools. Her research focuses on implementing human sexuality education and health education programs. She recently served on the eleven-member Governor's Red-Ribbon Panel on AIDS and was appointed to the State of Florida Department of Education Task Force for Developing Minimum Guidelines for Human Sexuality Education and HIV/AIDS Education.